In Favor of Growing Older

In Favor of Growing Older

*Guidelines and Practical Suggestions
for Planning Your Retirement Career*

Tilman R. Smith

Introduction by Thomas C. Cook, Jr.

HERALD PRESS
Scottdale, Pennsylvania
Kitchener, Ontario
1981

Library of Congress Cataloging in Publication Data

Smith, Tilman R., 1903-
In favor of growing older.

Bibliography: p.
1. Aged—United States. 2. Aging—Psychological aspects. 3. Maturation
(Psychology) I. Title.
HQ1064.U5S592   305.2'6   81-6996
ISBN 0-8361-1978-9 (pbk.)   AACR2

Scripture quotations in this book, unless otherwise noted, are from the
Revised Standard Version of the Bible, copyrighted 1946, 1952, © 1971, 1973.

IN FAVOR OF GROWING OLDER
Copyright © 1981 by Herald Press, Scottdale, Pa. 15683
Published simultaneously in Canada by Herald Press,
Kitchener, Ont. N2G 4M5
Library of Congress Catalog Card Number: 81-6996
International Standard Book Number: 0-8361-1978-9
Printed in the United States of America
Design by Tom Hershberger
Cover photo by M. Roessler from H. Armstrong Roberts

81 82 83 84 85 86 12 11 10 9 8 7 6 5 4 3 2 1

To Louella, my wife for nearly a half century; our children and their spouses: Carolyn and Tom, Marian and Dave, John and Joann, Eleanor, Stan and Rita; and our grandchildren—all of whom have made my life a joyful pilgrimage rather than a dull journey.

Contents

Author's Preface

The preacher in Ecclesiastes said 2200 years ago, "Of making many books there is no end; and much study is a weariness of the flesh" (Eccl. 12:12, KJV). What would the preacher say today? Until 1950, gerontology received little attention in research or reporting. However, since 1950 there has been an avalanche of research and writings. (Geriatrics, a branch of medicine dealing with diseases of older persons, should not be used synonymously with gerontology, which denotes the study of the aging process.)

From 1954 to 1974 more than 50,000 books and articles were printed dealing with gerontology. The logarithmic expansion of research continues and we are only beginning to scratch the surface in understanding aging.

—Diana S. Woodruff and James E. Birren in *Aging* (D. Van Nostrandt Co., 1975), p. 3

During the past twelve years I have developed a library on gerontology which now includes some 400 books, more than a dozen file drawers full of articles, and subscriptions to a dozen magazines on gerontology. I recognize that this is only a small sample, but a representative one, of what is available. I have attended and participated in many workshops on aging, including the 1971 White House Conference on Aging in Washington, D.C.

Why, then, another book on aging? Is it presumptuous for me to think I can expand the dimensions of gerontological knowledge? What new dimensions can I help bring into focus?

Three foci. I have tried, first of all, to present the material in this book in a manner which will be useful regardless of the age of the reader. Whatever our age, we must understand the maturation process or we will be overwhelmed physically, socially, emotionally, and spiritually as time moves on.

If you are young, you are determining now the kind of person you will be forty or fifty, sixty, or even seventy years from now. You take yourself with you as you grow older. What kind of an older person do you want to be? How you live now is the most important factor in determining how you grow older. Don't think of old age as a crisis, but as a natural stage in life.

If you are middle-aged, you and your peers are parents and teachers, decision makers, more likely to be established economically and participating in the power structures than younger people. If you don't plan now for retirement living, you may find your older years less fulfilling than they could have been. You can avoid many of the physical and mental problems of aging if you understand and follow the rules of the game.

If you are already an older person, it's not too late to learn. Your physical and mental health are at stake. Many services are available to you which can be helpful if you find out about them. Accept the fact that everyone sustains losses. Measure your success in coping by considering how well you are functioning with what you still have.

A second feature of this book is that it places priority on developing the resources within persons throughout life rather than emphasizing their problems and needs.

A third focus is the recognition that the church—its congregations and its institutions—is a new audience in the field of aging. In thinking of the aging process in the past, the church has dealt largely with building and operating residential homes for older persons. Nursing homes reach only 5 percent of those sixty-five and over. Little attention has been given to utilizing the resources and recognizing the basic needs of the 95 percent who are not institutionalized. This book recognizes that segment of the American population—over 24,000,000 persons—and offers suggestions for their continued involvement in positive and abundant living.

The religious sector prior to the decade of the 1970s has given scant and sporadic attention to the education of its constituencies in this crucial field of challenge and opportunity.
— *Theological Education* (Winter 1980), p. 307

Acknowledgments. I do not claim technical expertise in all of the fields which I've covered in this study. However, I feel more comfortable regarding this inadequacy since I have had the counsel of experts. A biologist, a physical education specialist, two medical doctors, an Old Order Amish historian and editor, an attorney, a dentist, several theologians, a sociologist, a psychologist, a nurse, an investment and estate planner, and a university demographer are among those who have advised me in their areas of expertise. I am fortunate and thankful to have had these unusual resources available.

Persons too numerous to mention by name have encouraged me in this project for a number of years. Some have sent me clippings or alerted me to materials for consideration. I thank each of them for their interest and goodwill.

From time to time task forces and ad hoc committees have made significant contributions to my efforts in studies and programs for the aging. I gratefully acknowledge their help. More specifically, I thank the Mennonite Board of Missions, Elkhart, Indiana, which gave encouragement, furnished personnel resources for this work, and approved the final manuscript.

The Health and Welfare Committee of the Mennonite Board of Missions gave constant encouragement, direction, and some gentle nudges toward consummation of the project. Its chairman, Willard Krabill, MD, deserves special recognition and thanks. Dr. Krabill shared helpful materials through the years, gave encouragement, carefully reviewed early drafts, recommended deletions and changes, and read the final manuscript with a trained eye. In addition, he wrote the chapter subsection on "Human Sexuality."

Thanks also to Evelyn Gunden, who spent many hours deciphering and typing the early drafts and the final manuscript. This was no easy task but an important one.

Luke Birky, secretary for the Health and Welfare Department until 1979, was a constant resource person and promoter for this book. His insights and good spirit were much appreciated. He also read the final manuscript.

Kenneth Schmidt, present director of the Health and Welfare Department, has given his blessing and encouragement.

Frances Greaser, a nurse and longtime member of the Health and Welfare Committee, and Marvin Nafziger of Mennonite Mutual Aid read the manuscript and gave good counsel.

John Rudy, general manager of Financial Services, Mennonite Mutual Aid, wrote the chapter subsection on "Financial

Planning" and assisted in other ways.

Beulah Kauffman, associate secretary for Congregational Family Life Education, Mennonite Board of Congregational Ministries until August 1980, was in a sense the final supervisor of the project. She helped prepare the final manuscript, arranged for its review, and kept in close contact with the editor and publisher.

I acknowledge especially the contribution of John Bender who served as editor of this book. During past years I spent much time gathering, researching, and writing articles on the aging process. However, without the invaluable services of an editor, it would have been difficult for me to choose from the materials produced and to put them into their present form.

In addition I wish to acknowledge the significant personal efforts of Paul M. Schrock, book editor at Herald Press, who gave a substantial block of time in reshaping the entire manuscript for the best possible acceptance.

To pinpoint the "always aging, ever living, mutual involvement" nature of every person's life, John Bender suggested the "Involvement" feature at the end of each chapter and personally made some of the investigations. He also developed the discussion and action starters which appear at the end of each chapter.

Intended audiences. *In Favor of Growing Older* will be helpful to persons in a variety of settings: ministers, the enablers in the congregation; local church boards; congregational committees on aging; Sunday school teachers (discussion questions and action starters at the end of each chapter make the book useful as a Sunday school elective); and Christian schools (including seminaries interested in training ministers how to deal with the issues of aging).

The book may also interest persons in public schools, especially social studies teachers; administrators and staff members of nursing and retirement homes; community social agencies with programs for older persons; and community, industrial, and religious continuing education leaders.

—Tilman R. Smith
Goshen, Indiana

Introduction

A poster in my office reads: "We old folks know more about being young than you young folks know about being old." Too many well-meaning writers on aging are peddling advice which, no matter how logical or informative, turns out to resemble a travelogue given by one who has never made the trip.

Author Tilman Smith and I agree on the kind and quality of book on aging much needed in the community of faith. Among the many good books that have appeared in recent years, *In Favor of Growing Older* is distinctively organized, holistic in content, and positively hopeful about the aging process. The pages are indelibly marked by Tilman Smith's 78 years of experience, research, wisdom, and personal understanding of the subject of aging.

While aging is a process from conception to death and therefore of relevance to all of us, the pages of this book are much like a letter of hope to those facing, or now in, the later years. Today's older adults are different from those of a generation or two ago. Looking ahead a few years, those of us in our middle years and, of course, our children and grandchildren, will be different too.

But important to every generation is how to negotiate life now. What is there to guide us through unchartered waters? If we are to discard old negative myths about growing older, what new understandings of aging can we live with? One recent writer suggests that religion poses the alternative. "Religion tells us that everyday reality is indeed untrue and invalid, a swindle unless it is invaded and transfigured by the sacred. Faith in another reality offers an alternative framework to which the self may be attached."[1] By faith, timeless unchanging values make each day in the believer's life a victory, dispelling any notion of returning to either the "good old days" or of deferring our life satisfaction and well-being to that nebulous "by-and-by" when time shall be no more. Our spiritual well-being will be qualified by what and in whom we believe. For Christians and Jews alike, we have God's Word that the later years are a part of his eternal creative order. That means as we grow older we dare not seek to escape the kind of involvement to which these chapters call us.

The recent White House Conference on Aging will be making its imprint on American policy on aging for some years to come. However, unless its concerns include the spiritual well-being of older persons, it will not meet the needs of the whole person. While public attention to aging is important, ethical, moral, and spiritual issues in our aging society must also find their resolution in the household of faith.

In Favor of Growing Older calls us to discard and refute anything in our culture that robs us of human dignity, usefulness, and service. In positive fashion, Smith helps us recognize that God, in creating us in his own image, surely did not intend us to spend the last third of life in useless idleness or frustrated despair. Nor can we find any evidence here that God favors the trend toward isolating older people from general society. Rather, the truth of our Hebrew-Christian faith is an ever-present theme: every individual is worthy in the sight of God and growing older is a part of his plan for us throughout eternity. Today, as in every age, we must champion the dispossessed, the poor, the disabled. But something is different. Because we are living longer and enjoying better health, both the church and the individual believer must come to grips with the meaning of life beyond the productive working years.

The National Interfaith Coalition on Aging, with which I am identified, has defined spiritual well-being as "the affirmation of life in a relationship with God, self, community, and environment that celebrates and nurtures wholeness."[2] In our growing, changing, pluralistic world, spiritual well-being is found only in a community that has "caught on" to that which is eternal. Most of us share the prophetic dream of a community formed around unchanging, transcendent, but relevant, values. We need a community today which cannot be destroyed by socio-economic roller coasters and current events. The writer to the Hebrews tells of Abraham "seeking a city which has foundations whose builder and maker is God" (Heb. 11:10). Zechariah foresees a time "in the faithful city" when men and women of ripe old age will sit in the city squares and the streets will be full of boys and girls playing there (Zech. 8:1-5). Getting ourselves ready for that kind of

---

1. Elizabeth Janeway, Review of *The Coming of Age. Atlantic Monthly.* 229:94-98, 1972.

2. "Spiritual Well-being," National Interfaith Coalition on Aging, 1975.

fulfillment requires not only knowledge of gerontology and the best that scientists and legislators can give us, but essential human values and the faith, hope, and love which must characterize all we do in the name of Jesus Christ.

The decades of the 1960s and 1970s saw profound modifications in the values and belief systems of our society, especially those having to do with the changing roles of women and men, family structure, attitudes toward the young and old, and changes in the modes and fashion of worship. Aging, for all of the recent attention to it, is still new to today's world. The danger is that while we explode one set of myths, we may forge new stereotypes for the next generation to disprove. What was normative for our grandparents—in life expectancy, health, economics of retirement, mobility, and family relationships—no longer applies to today's older people. Nor will what seems self-evident to us about aging hold up long for future generations. Other variables create crosscurrents of change. Unforeseen inflation has suddenly eroded life savings, limited housing choices and travel opportunities, and undercut nutrition, health, and bodily comfort for many in our day.

Part of our task is to cope with change with the tools of faith. But we must also recognize the unchanging principles that enable us to participate in life and contribute to the whole community that which is uniquely the gift of the years. The Apostle Paul told the believers in Thessalonica that he did not want them to be "ignorant about death." Neither are believers to be ignorant or fearful about growing older. The church can shoulder its responsibilities by equipping the saints for living life to the full all the days of our life. Tilman Smith has called us to that task and set before us achievable goals, practical steps, and parallel resources in an excellent volume. Read on!

—Thomas C. Cook, Jr.
Executive Director
National Interfaith Coalition
on Aging (NICA)

Your Mind Can Sharpen with Age

"Who wants to be ninety-one?" a young man of nineteen asked with a sneer. "I do," replied a ninety-year-old man modestly. Most of us want to live a long time but we don't want to grow old.

The ninety-year-old man spoke in favor of living. It's as though he had said, "I belong here. I want to live a long physical life not because I dread death, but because new horizons are the birthright of older persons as well as the young. I want to live in joy and peace and help to create joy and peace for others. I anticipate a further grand transition, borne in the pain and separation of death, yet with the certainty of an alternative to life that means new life. Right now, though, I want to go on living."

A ninety-year-old person can look ahead, guided by the vision of a today worth living and a tomorrow worth anticipating. It's a birthright. The days ahead, whether you're nineteen or ninety-one, can be the best part of your life, if you put your heart, years, and mind to it. Life is for living.

Myth 1: Growing old comes by getting older

One can live a long time without growing old. In general, our mind, not our physical body, determines our age.

The human brain does not shrink, wilt, perish, or deteriorate with age. It normally continues to function well through as many as nine decades.
—Alex Comfort in *A Good Age* (Crown, 1976), p. 45.

The mind is generally the last part of the body to wear out. Some superb physical specimens may be intellectual and social dwarfs who grow old early while others with weak bodies and disciplined minds may never know old age even though they reach the tenth decade.

An unknown author wrote: "Nobody grows old by merely living a number of years. People grow old only by deserting their ideals. Years may wrinkle the skin but to give up interest shrivels the soul. In the central place of every heart there is a recording chamber; so long as it receives messages of beauty, hope, cheer, and courage, you are young. When the wires are down and your heart is covered with the snows of pessimism and the ice of cynicism, then and only then have you grown old."

Many young and middle-aged persons and also some elders have unrealistic fears about the aging process. They call to mind persons who are physically decrepit, senile, dependent, lonely and poor, the extremely frail and vulnerable who are unable to fend for themselves. Admittedly, such persons need our support, love, and medical attention—not our scorn or neglect. The senile and decrepit, however, are only a small percent of the 25,000,000 people in the United States who are over sixty-five. From this small group we form stereotype images of aging, and our fears turn into obsessions. We overreact to the reality of aging and try cheap cover-ups such as "Hate that gray, wash it away," "Look like a bride again," and "Try wrinkle cream." We swallow capsules to take care of ourselves. We attempt other silly accommodations to our past, fearful that the future holds less than we deserve.

Myth 2: It would be better to be younger than you are

Several years ago I attended a workshop in which we were asked to write the answers to three questions: How old would you like to be at this time? How old would you like to have other people think you are? How old are you? I was comfortable to record the same figure for each question. Jonathan Swift (1667-1745), English satirist, said, "No wise man ever wished to be younger." Another person commented, "I don't want to be young again. If you do it right, once is enough."

> **Would I wish to be "young" again? No, for I have
> learned too much to wish to lose it. It would be like failing
> to pass a grade in school. I have reached an honorable
> position in life, because I am old and no longer young. I am
> a far more valuable person today than I was 50 years ago,
> or 40 years ago, or 30, 20, or even 10. I HAVE LEARNED
> SO MUCH SINCE I WAS 70! I believe that I can honestly
> say that I have learned more in the last 10 years than I
> have learned in any previous decade. This, I suppose, is
> because I have perfected my techniques, so that I no
> longer waste time in learning how to do what I have to do.**
> —The late Pearl S. Buck in her "Essay on Life," written at
> age 79

A middle-aged housewife reported to a small group that a younger person asked her, "Don't you wish you were young again?" She answered, "Do you mean to rear a family again; to follow my kids around all day, change their diapers, go through all those experiences of adolescence, put them through college? I guess not!"

Myth 3: Intelligence declines with age

It has been drilled into our minds that there's no good reason for older persons to try to keep on learning because the effort isn't worthwhile—you reach the law of diminishing returns. Nonsense. We have been too willing to settle for the shibboleth that an older dog can't learn new tricks. We have assumed that mental decline and aging are synonymous. It just isn't so, even though past methods of intelligence testing reinforce the fiction.

Intelligence tests historically were made for the younger members of the test group based on current data, not cross-generational in nature. The investigators administered to persons of various ages a test slanted to the younger age group and then compared their performance levels. Many studies of this type conducted during the thirties, forties, and fifties led the researchers to believe that intelligence increases up to early adulthood, reaches a plateau that lasts for about ten years, and then begins to decline in a predictable pattern in the fourth decade of life. The error in the old intelligence test postulates came to light with a new approach to testing.

Longitudinal tests. Other researchers began to realize that the environment and the cultural climate of each generation were different and concluded that tests which compared different generations gave inaccurate answers. Accordingly, they concluded that longitudinal tests, which compared individuals with themselves over the years, would more nearly indicate individual abilities. Much research of this type has been carried on more recently.

Paul B. Baltes and K. Warner Schaie in 1956 tested 500 subjects ranging in age from twenty-one to seventy. Seven years later they retested 301 of the same subjects with the same tests and found that intelligence need not slide downhill from adulthood to old age. By many measures it increases. They discovered that the old man's boast, "I'm as good as I ever was," may be true, and that intelligence during maturity and old age does not decline as soon as people had earlier assumed.
—Reported in "Aging and IQ—The Myth of the Twilight Years" *Psychology Today* (March 1974), copyright 1974, Ziff Davis Publishing Co.

The tests—don't let the technical terms derail you—were divided into the following areas:

—*crystalized intelligence,* which encompasses the sorts of skills one acquires through education, in acculturization such as verbal comprehension, numerical skills, and inductive reasoning;

—*cognitive flexibility,* which measures the ability to shift from one way of thinking to another within the context of familiar intellectual operations;

—*visuomotor flexibility,* which measures a similar but independent skill, the one involved in shifting familiar to unfamiliar patterns, tasks requiring coordination between visual and motor abilities; and

—*verbalization,* which measures the ability to organize and process visual materials and involves tasks such as finding a simple figure contained in a complex one or identifying a picture that is incomplete.

When the results were looked at longitudinally, comparing a given age-group performance in 1956 with its performance in 1963, a *definite decline was found in only one of the four measures:* visuomotor flexibility. Even people over seventy improved from the first testing to the second.

In addition, the ability of elderly people to memorize and recall new information has been tested by Duke University Center for the Study of Aging and Human Development. The conclusion was that older persons have a good ability to learn new things but they need more time than younger people. Their responses are apparently slowed by anxiety. An older person's goal is less to achieve success than to avoid failure. Changes in the blood pressure of elderly persons showed that they were undergoing the physiological equivalent of anxiety without being aware of it when taking tests. Dr. Carl Eisendorfer, who conducted the experiment, suggested that what initially slowed down his subjects was not so much their age as their attitude toward their age.

Other studies. Some other studies show a comparable increase in capability in doing some intellectual tasks as persons get older.

In Scotland 141 postgraduate teachers, average persons, were tested in 1930-1934, average age of 22½. These persons were retested in 1955, 25 years later at age 47. The test had 14 components. These persons in general showed increases in all 14 subtests; 13 of them were statistically significant. Improvement was less marked in numerical than in the verbal area.
   —Jack Botwinick in *Cognitive Processes in Maturity and Old Age*

In 1919, 363 male freshmen at Iowa State, Ames, Iowa, were tested. Thirty years later (1949), 127 of the same subjects were retested. Four of the tests revealed no appreciable change, but four other tests showed increases in achievement. Thirteen years later (1962), 97 of the 127 were retested at an average age of sixty-one. A plateau had been reached. In numerical areas of the test, there was some decline. However, Professor Owens, one of the testers, was much more impressed with the general lack of decline than in the one component—numerical—which did fall off with age. Longtime exposure can equalize different abilities such as overall wisdom, overall insight, and the ability to cope.

Potential for growth. Can everyone expect to become brighter and sweeter as the years roll by? Not necessarily; it depends on how we use our gifts. Initial ability is crucial. A bright seventy-year-old person was still sharper than an average twenty-year-old. Verbal, practical, affective [emotional and feeling], cognitive, and social skills may better describe an adult's mental ability than scores which can be converted from an IQ test. Often decline may be due to environmental factors such as a dull, repetitive job. We should also realize that most tests deal more with "school learning" than with problem solving. Intelligence and the ability to learn are not the same thing. Except for deteriorating illness (mental or physical) and the failure to discipline and use our minds, we can continue to grow.

Older people not only retain the capacity to learn, their levels of intellectual performance can measurably improve in the proper settings. In the proper educational settings older people's performances improve if they are allowed as much time as they want to complete a learning task. In fact, Eisendorfer found that increased time to complete a task improves older people's performances to a greater degree than for young people. The most effective learning environment for the elderly appears to be one which combines auditory and visual information, frequent repetition, a leisurely pace, and rewards.
—James D. Manney, Jr., in *Aging in American Society*

Myth 4: Forgetting is a sign of senility

Frequently we hear younger and middle-aged persons say: "I must be getting senile; I forget so often." But instances of temporary memory loss come to all ages. A forty-five-year-old man attempted to introduce his son-in-law to me and forgot his name. In a group meeting of institutional administrators who were introducing themselves and giving their church affiliation, a young man could not think of the church body with which he was associated. An ABC sports announcer one time temporarily forgot his own name in a TV announcement. We tend to overlook this kind of *faux pas* with younger persons but assume it is the heritage of older persons.

> **I lose my glasses five times a day and nobody says I'm senile. But if somebody old does, everyone gets hysterical. However, as you can't tell a child there is no monster under the bed, you can't brush off a person's concern about senility.**
> —James Folsom, Veterans Administration, in *The National Observer* (March 31, 1973)

Persons of all ages forget. Older persons probably forget recent events more frequently, not as a result of approaching senility, but out of a habit that can be changed.

> ***Question:*** **Lately I find it hard to remember. What could be the reason and what can I do to improve my memory?**
> ***Answer:*** **Memory loss can be caused by a beginning obstruction of the arteries to the brain. This is related to stroke. A more probable cause of memory loss is inattention. It is a common human characteristic as people grow older to pay little or no attention to what goes on around them or to what people say to them. The result is a deprived input into their memory bank. They develop the inability to recall things they should know about and at the time and instance something occurs it does not register. This can be corrected by a conscious effort to be aware of what is going on around you.**
> —From *More Life for Your Years* (September 1972), copyright 1972, American Medical Association

Most of us have not perfected the skill of listening and we spend little time trying to improve this ability. It is particularly important for older persons, whose physical senses may be somewhat impaired, to give special attention to noticing what's going on around them.

Myth 5: Losing brain cells diminishes thinking power

It is true that the brain loses cells each day and may even get physically smaller. However, in comparison to the fifteen or twenty billion brain cells with which we are originally endowed, such losses are negligible. Yet, if the brain does tend to melt away some, how can we think as well or better than we did fifteen or twenty years ago?

Most older persons have accumulated knowledge and wisdom. They have developed patterns of thinking which often enhance brain activity with age. These factors may more than offset the steady loss of cells. Since thinking is a skill and not simply a matter of the number of cells in the brain, organized thinking processes are the key to efficient brain activity. Also, most of us have mental potential which we do not use. This reserve is available for use if we but call upon it.

One persistent bit of folklore about the brain is that we lose a vast number of brain cells as we grow old and senility is often associated with the shrinkage of brain tissue and the loss of brain cells; many people assume that mental and physical deterioration are the inevitable companions of aging. As a neuroanatomist I have been intrigued by this myth of the disappearing brain cells especially because the fact "has a sinister side." It lends a spurious air of scientific validity to our practice of relegating old people to empty, meaningless lives. When I search the scientific literature I fail to find a single thorough study which showed changes in the brain cell counts of mammals as they age.

Conversely, it seems clear that inactivity is detrimental to the brain capacity of people as well as rats. The worst thing we can do is to consign elderly people to sedentary confinement in an unstimulating nursing home. To do so is to perpetuate the fallacy that brain cell loss and mental deterioration inevitably accompany old age.

—Marion C. Diamond, Professor of Anatomy at the University of California, Berkeley, in "Aging and Cell Loss: Calling for an Honest Count" *(Psychology Today,* September, 1978), p. 126, copyright 1978, Ziff Davis Publishing Co.

Myth 6: To age is to become senile

For many years it was expected that older persons would lose command of their mental faculties as they grew older. Every act somewhat deviant from expected behavior was labeled senile. The experts held out little hope.

"The prognosis of senile psychoses is manifestly hopeless. No well-defined remissions are to be expected. The course is progressive, the patient is gradually becoming more and more demented although life may continue ten years or even longer before death supervenes," A. P. Noyes reported in 1939 in *Modern Clinical Psychiatry.* This insidious and erroneous concept is still with us today and too often rules our thinking.

Senility is an invention of modern Western society. It is one of the most damaging self-fulfilling prophecies ever devised. Persons who are told by doctors that they are senile even without any understanding of the term believe that they are finished and act accordingly.
—Douglas S. Looney in *The National Observer* (March 31, 1973)

What is senility? Senility "is the deterioration of the intellectual capacity," James W. Warren, MD, editor of *Health Digest,* reported in the October 1978 issue. "The earliest symptoms often go unnoticed and include such things as slight loss of mental quickness, memory, and initiative. The person seems to lose interest in life and seems slower. The symptoms often are mistaken for fatigue or boredom and in many instances depression or boredom are mistaken for senility. The next noticeable signs are a loss in recent memory and difficulties in speech. While a person may be able to clearly remember things from the past he or she often cannot remember what happened yesterday or even an hour ago. There also may be episodes of bizarre behavior like undressing at inappropriate times, forgetting where one is and neglecting personal cleanliness. In severe cases the victim of true senility is unable to function on his own and must be cared for."

These are the classic signs of senile dementia. Similar symptoms may be caused by a number of disorders, however, many of which can be treated. Dr. Warren cites examples such as tumors, hypothyroidism, nutritional deficiencies, infections such as syphilis, and misuse of certain drugs such as alcohol or barbiturates as producing symptoms which mimic senility. That is why it is important to conduct certain tests before concluding that the patient is indeed senile. The diagnosis should be confirmed by a geriatric specialist.

In the same article Dr. Leo Hollister, a leading psychiatrist at Stanford University, said, "Thousands of elderly Americans are relegated to a vegetable-like existence simply because we assume there is nothing we can do to help them. In reality, many if not most of these people can be helped by an accurate diagnosis and an early treatment of the problem."

Senility is not an inevitable consequence of growing old; in fact, it is not even a disease. . . . Rather, "senility" is a word commonly used to described a large number of conditions with an equally large number of causes, many of which respond to prompt and effective treatment.
— *Special Report on Aging* (National Institutes of Health, 1979), p. 2

How common is de facto senility? Dr. Robert N. Butler, a specialist in mental diseases of the aged and director of the National Institute on Aging, has pointed out that as many as one out of 23 older Americans may have some form of intellectual dysfunction that may be labeled senility. Even of the existing cases half may be reversible or at least treatable. According to Dr. Butler, a hundred or more conditions can cause pseudo-senility, including anemia, dehydration, congestive heart failure, and mild infections.

Another common cause of pseudo-senility is depression which also can be treated but is often neglected in the elderly. Most experts agree that senility is not inevitable. Dr. Leslie Libow, medical director of the Jewish Institute for Geriatric Care in Long Island, New York, summed up the views of many by saying senility is not a natural phenomenon like the graying of the hair.

Experts also agree that the best way to maintain mental and physical health is to stay active. Dr. Butler said, "The older people I see who remain in the best shape are those who have taken the least drugs and who drink very, very little alcohol." Dr. Libow added, "If one's day is repetitive and unvaried there seems to be a higher correlation with bodily decline." So a varied and complex day is one common-sense and apparently scientifically valid approach to maintaining health in old age.

Misdiagnosis. Lawrence Galton reports that misdiagnosis of senility blights the last years of many with treatable ailments. He gives these examples:

The eighty-five-year-old man was a pitiable sight. Brought in to the Jewish Institute for Geriatric Care in New Hyde Park, New York, he could only slump in a chair, eyelids drooping, hands trembling, mumbling answers to questions, wearing three sweaters to keep warm.

Although he had been repeatedly diagnosed as senile elsewhere, physicians of the facility refused to write him off. The three sweaters provided a clear clue. A blood test quickly confirmed the suspicion. The old man was suffering from acute thyroid deficiency in which low body heat is one major symptom. With daily thyroid hormone treatment, his senility cleared rapidly.

In Florida a seventy-two-year-old woman was hospitalized because of increased severe memory loss and confusion. Despite two weeks of intensive testing physicians could find nothing to explain her condition. Before labeling her senile, Dr. H. Gordon J. Gilbert of the University of South Florida Medical School checked her medical history. Fourteen years before she had suffered a heart attack. Ever since then she had been taking large doses of quinidine sulfate to keep her heart rhythm normal. The heart was fine. But suspicious of the heavy continued use of quinidine Dr. Gilbert discontinued it. Within 48 hours she had recovered and could be discharged.

—Lawrence Galton in *Parade Magazine* (November 4, 1979)

Social relationships often at the root of senility. In the 1971 White House Conference on Aging study guide, *Spiritual Well-Being* (p. 7), Philip L. White, then secretary-director of the Department of Foods and Nutrition, American Medical Association, said: "Senility is frequently, if not always, the consequence of social relationships which produce anxiety and overtax the older person's ability to function. Psychosomatic ailments are widespread among the elderly, although frequently they are not diagnosed as such because of the assumption that the conditions are inevitable consequences of aging. The personal habits of some aged people which make them revolting to others can similarly be traced to problems of social relationships."

White added, "Food is associated with love so when an older person feels rejected, shut out, unloved, and socially isolated his eating habits are affected. He begins to subsist on toast and tea, loses weight and winds up in a hospital or nursing home."

In the book, *The Daily Needs and Interests of Older People,* Adeline Hoffman editor (p. 130), Maurice Linden records experimental treatment for senile persons which he carried out. He treated 51 female patients. Three were younger than sixty and one was eighty-nine. The time spent in the hospital before treatment ranged from one month to forty years. The average was about four years and ten months. Thirty-one had been hospitalized for two years or less.

Patients were classified as much, moderately, or slightly improved or showing no change whatever. None became worse. Of the total group the results were 22 patients were much improved; eight were moderately improved; eleven showed slight improvement and only ten were unchanged. Twenty-three persons or forty-five percent of the total left the hospital for their own homes, county homes, or placements. A rough comparison was made of those results with the other 279 patients in the same building who did not participate in therapy. Of the latter only 13 percent left the hospital compared with 45 percent of the therapy group. The results, while inconclusive and subject to some question, do point out that there seems to be a relationship between the attitudes of responsible health personnel and the fates of the aged ill.

Senility in younger persons. *Time* Magazine (August 13, 1970, "The Old in the Country of the Young") reported: "Actually senile traits are not peculiar to the aged. A group of college students and a group of the elderly were recently graded according to the characteristics of senility and the students were found to be more neurotic, negative, dissatisfied, socially inept, and unrealistic. The students in some ways were more senile than their elders. Other studies have shown that the percentage of psychiatric impairment of older persons is no greater than that for younger persons."

In an interview with Dr. Frances M. Carp of Wright Institute, Berkeley, California, March 1974, Dr. Carp told the writer that she gave identical senility tests to college sophomores and a group of older persons, and found more senile characteristics in the sophomores. These statements do not imply there is no senility among older persons but rather that we should not label every lapse of memory (or even stupid acts) as symptoms of senility. Persons need to recognize the difference between what can and cannot be controlled. Care of truly mentally impaired persons calls for a loving response. Prevention, on the other hand, calls for an equal initiative.

I think some people have been born senile. They never get an original thought. They don't grab life; they let life grab them. To prevent becoming senile:
1. **Be active.**
2. **Eat properly.**
3. **Be interested.**
4. **Be smart.**
5. **Control stress.**
6. **Get adequate sleep.**
7. **Give yourself pep talks.**
8. **Learn new skills.**
9. **Think in terms of second and third careers.**
10. **Don't get fat.**
11. **Do things for others.**
12. **Never say, "I'm too old."**
13. **Don't fret about memory lapses.**
14. **Don't think you're becoming stupid.**
15. **Don't give up things in the name of "I'm getting old and forgetful."**
16. **Inspire yourself.**
17. **Curb your anxieties.**
   —Douglas S. Looney in *The National Observer* (March 31, 1973)

The above suggestions may seem rather glib and easier said than done. However, they do indicate a climate and frame of reference from which we may be able to select some helpful hints at whatever age we may be.

Myth 7: An old dog can't learn new tricks

We should recognize that some slowing does come with age with reference to our ability to learn. However, this is not particularly significant. By keeping their brain in practice, older persons can think just as well as when they were younger, even though not as rapidly. They still have the capacity to learn virtually anything they choose to learn and think worthwhile. They may give up easier and have less ability to produce energy sufficient to meet stressful conditions. But, learn they can. A satisfying physical, mental, emotional, and spiritual life is possible for the majority of older persons if society finds value in providing a reasonable framework in which they can live and work.

Older persons' reactions are apt to come more slowly than the responses of younger persons, and the very old are often very slow in word and deed. It takes time to search through the accumulated knowledge and wisdom of many years and sort out the best answers, discarding those solutions which have been tried and found wanting. Many of us in our mad dash to live have missed, for want of waiting, the answers which have been tested and have a good chance of contributing to solutions for all of us.

And so we come to the general conclusion that an old dog can learn new tricks but the answer is not a direct and simple one. It appears that the old dog is reluctant to learn tricks. He is less likely to gamble on the results particularly when he is not convinced that the new trick is any better than the old trick that served him so well in the past. He may not learn the new trick as rapidly as he did in the past but learn it, he does. Further, if evidence seems to be that he starts out as a clever young pup, he is very likely to end up a very wise old hound.

—Ledford J. Bischof in *Adult Psychology* (Harper & Row, 1969), p. 221

INVOLVEMENT: Writing poetry in a nursing home

Some residents of a nursing home in Elkhart, Indiana, found they could give poetic expression to their thoughts and experiences with a little help from some Goshen College friends. Student Carl Haarer originally led the group until his graduation. Another student, Shari Miller, continued the weekly experience. She describes the involvement:

We call ourselves "Poetry Corner" and although a corner of the lounge is our physical domain, our poetic kingdom spreads over starfish and cities, peacocks and dreams.

Many people have the mistaken notion that a poem is

not a poem unless it rhymes. That is unfortunate—for a poem is, foremost of all, an expression of abstract feelings and ideas in concrete terms. This definition of poetry is one which allows us to write in free verse fashion. Our process is simple. First I introduce the topic or ask for a suggestion. Our subjects have ranged from silence to crazy quilts and from September to nightmares. Sometimes I stimulate the imagination by reading a poem by a well-known poet, or I show them an actual object (such as a peacock feather or a seashell). Within one or two minutes the lines begin coming, and I can hardly move my pen fast enough.

As the group tells me their poem, I am careful to read it back to them about every five lines; that way they are reminded that they are, indeed, composing a poem and not simply a conversation. The next week I return with the poem typed and a copy for each poet. "Did we write that?" they often say. "Why, that's pretty good."

Before my first session with the group, I was under the misconception that these people would probably be cloudy-minded—senile—perhaps out of touch with the "real" world. How wrong I was! I have found the group to be intelligent, witty, wise, and imaginative. But what I've come to value most of all is their truthfulness. They have no "image" to protect; they are vulnerable and willing to take risks—whether with the playing of words or with the sharing of memories from their past.

Although I hope that the workshop is one way to help the group stay in touch with a world of snowflakes and sunshine, our poetry is *not* "therapy." It is an artistic endeavor and that's how we treat it. Here's one of our creations:

AND WE ASK, WHY, WHY?

*I can think of oodles of questions
But finding the answers is another story.*

*I could never understand why chickens' heads
go back and forth when they walk.
I've wondered: why, why?
They have two legs like people.
Maybe it's good;
Some of us don't use our heads.*

*Why do you shovel snow?
Why do we have snow?
To wade through?
To see how deep it can get?*

And why is the sky blue?
They say green is easier on the eyes.

Right now I'm wondering
If they'll ever make a car that has no noise.
Will electric cars hum?

How do they make raisins from grapes?
When you think about it, it's queer.

I wonder who invented the TV?
And why, why?
It's like why they invented the light bulb.

—By the Class (October 22, 1979)

Some of the money from two of the group's published poems was used for a party complete with a violinist who played Irish tunes. With the rest of the money they bought a dictionary for the nursing home.

Persons interested in beginning a workshop for older people in poetry reading will find excellent guidance in Kenneth Koch's book, *I Never Told Anybody ... Teaching Poetry Writing in a Nursing Home* (Random House, 1977).

STARTERS

1
Call your parents, write a letter; for no reason send flowers with a note, "Love you, mom and dad. Looking forward to being with you on Thanksgiving—Jim, Sue, and the kids."

2
Take a leisurely trip with your retired parents, maybe to a place the family visited thirty years ago. Try new places, too. Include day picnics in your annual schedule. On extended trips provide for each person to be alone one hour each day. Share in daily devotional experiences.

3
Include a story time in seasonal family gatherings, complete with old movies, some slides, and lots of "Grandma, tell us about your courtship days, school days, recreation...." Unplug the TV and plug in the tape recorder.

4
Encourage older persons to pursue interests in intergenerational groups as well as in clubs or groups of their own. Choirs, college classes, serving as resource persons for youth groups, and foster grandparenting help oldsters maintain a sense of extended family and allow them to contribute and grow. Maybe all that's lacking is a ride to and from the event—or help with grooming, such as combing their hair.

5
Invite a qualified speaker to a special conference for middle-aged and older persons to sharpen understanding of the way verbal, practical, affective, cognitive, and social skills often increase with age.

6
Anticipate the warm, caring presence and reassurance that an older person needs in responding to severe losses. Be ready to show interest and care that understands and helps the person to make transitions. Communicate to the person, "I want you to enjoy being ninety-one."

7
Don't accept as subhuman the minority of elders who are as fragile and alone as the last leaf of fall. Find out what good nursing homes are doing in the care and stimulation of such persons. Plan a similar approach. Get involved.

2 Improve Your Chances for Good Health

"Fifty percent of the deaths today are premature and are the result of poor health practices and inferior living styles," the Surgeon General of the United States declared in an NBC broadcast in July 1979. "Smoking is the single most significant poor health practice. We don't do much to promote good health practices and spend little time in preventive health maintenance. We wait until a health crisis emerges and then we seek medical help."

Physical health

Many scientists in the field of human biology believe that a healthy infant should live to be a hundred years or more.

Most recent scientific observations indicate that, contrary to general belief, each person has an inborn potential to live past 100 years, and that each person, even if he has short-lived parents, can live up to his potential of 100 years of healthy, vigorous, active life.
—Quoted from the Gerontology Center at the University of California in *Retirement Living* (December, 1975), p. 24

Charlie Smith of Bartow, Florida, died October 5, 1979, at the age of 137. According to Social Security records he was the oldest person in the United States. Newspaper accounts indicate he was brought to the States as a slave from Liberia before the Civil War.

The U.S. Department of Health, Education, and Welfare in a *Special Report on Aging: 1979* said, "When our nation was founded—just a little over two hundred years ago—only 20 percent of newborns survived into old age (65). Today the reverse is true: 80 percent of newborns survive into old age while only 20 percent do not."

It is generally believed that the human lifespan, of about 100 years, has not changed since recorded history, but what has changed is the larger number of people surviving toward this apparent limit. Deaths in the early years are becoming increasingly less frequent. . . . In many underprivileged countries, one can now reasonably expect to become old, which is a very new phenomenon, indeed.
—Physiogerontologist Leonard Hayflick in *Extending the Human Life Span: Social Policy and Social Ethics*, p. 1

Quantity and quality go hand in hand. Gains in the quantity of life are not important unless the quality of life continues to improve in the later years. Benjamin Franklin once said, "A good life may not be long enough and a long life may not be good enough." The Bible includes long lists of genealogies telling who begat whom but little else about some lives.

The oldest person listed in the Bible has a short obituary: "Thus all the days of Methuselah were 969 years; and he died" (Gen. 5:27). In contrast his father, Enoch (Gen. 5:22-24), lived only a bit more than a third of Methuselah's years but his life history was recorded in more detail.

The New Testament comments, "By faith Enoch was taken up so that he should not see death; and he was not found, because God had taken him. Now before he was taken he was attested as having pleased God. And without faith it is impossible to please him" (Heb. 11:5, 6a).

To beget children is no great achievement. Preteenagers are doing that at an alarming rate in America. But to live a life pleasing to God has genuine significance.

Moses lived 120 years. His service during his last forty years, after he had turned eighty, was so significant that upon his death Israel had a national memorial service that lasted for thirty days: "His eye was not dim, nor his natural force abated. And the people of Israel wept for Moses in the plains of Moab thirty days; then the days of weeping and mourning for Moses were ended" (Deut. 34:7a, 8).

Aging is not a disease. Eighty-five percent of retired persons are in remarkably good health, live independently, have a reasonably good income due chiefly to government help, travel, pursue hobbies, read, enjoy friends, and in general get along well on their own. However, some older persons have chronic health problems and disabilities, and they need a doctor's services more often than younger persons. But sickness is something quite apart from aging.

Health defined. The World Health Organization defines health as "a state of total physical, psychological, sociological, and environmental well-being, and not only the absence of disease."

Every area of our life must be positively geared to living fruitfully and effectively without succumbing to negative, meaningless, and unhappy approaches. Too many of us have failed to understand and respect our bodies. Our physical and mental health is personal but not private. We are not our own. The Apostle Paul reminds us, "You were bought with a price" (1 Cor. 7:23a).

Others have invested in us. Many persons (particularly our parents, but also the church and the community) have invested much in us. If we waste our physical resources through profligate living, or through misuse or disuse, we sin. Abusing and destroying our bodies and minds knowingly or through ignorance shortcircuits our gifts and we are less than we should be. Unhealthful lifestyles may contribute to our becoming community liabilities rather than assets.

Respect your body. A doctor from New Orleans paid a beautiful tribute to the human body and the care and awe which we owe this marvel of creation.

MY BODY
Thank you, God, for this body.
For the things it can feel—
The things it can sense,
Thank you for the wondrous things it can do.

For the bright figure of my body at the day's beginning.
For its weariness at the day's end.
Thank you even for its pain—
If only to sting me into awareness of my own existence
                    upon earth.
I look upon your creation in amazement.
For we are indeed fearfully and wonderfully made.
All its secret, silent machinery—the meshing and churning—
What a miracle of design!
Don't let me hurt it, God.
Or scar it, or spoil it.
Or overindulge or overdrive it.
But don't let me coddle it, either, God.
Let me love my body enough to keep it agile.
And able, and well and strong.
            —Dr. Alton Ochsner

A California health study. The California Health Department's Human Population Committee began a long-term study of 7,000 residents in Alameda County in 1965, which continues today. Some recommendations emerged that are so simple many people will not accept their significance. Overall, the study indicates that following seven simple rules of clean living can add eleven years to the life of a man and seven years to that of a woman. The rules are:

1. **Get the right amount of sleep—eight hours a night for men, seven hours for women.**
2. **Eat a good breakfast each day.**
3. **Eat three meals a day at regular times and avoid snacks.**
4. **Exercise regularly, preferably by participating in sports.**
5. **Control your weight.**
6. **Drink moderately.***
7. **Don't smoke cigarettes.***
            —From an article, "Exercise, Clean Living Add Years to Life,"
            in *Newsletter of the President's Council on Physical Fitness
            and Sports* (January 1976)

*In reporting scientific studies, we must record the data as it was disclosed. I would suggest that nonuse is the direction toward which the church and society should be working. O. Quentin Hydar, MD, said in *Psychology for Living,* June 1978, "There is no safe 'level of drinking' because individuals differ widely in their vulnerability. Although total abstention is the perfect standard, Christians who drink are obligated to be strict with their own self-discipline. We are in danger of losing the protection and guiding influence of the Holy Spirit."

Nedra Belloc, MD, one of the authors of the California health study report, said that a man of forty-five who observes six or all of the rules can expect to live on the average to age seventy-nine; the man who observes three or fewer rules will be fortunate to reach sixty-seven. The findings that men can increase longevity by eleven years by following good health practices is especially significant since the life expectancy of adult men increased by only three years from 1900 to 1970. Our spectacular gains in longevity expectations (forty-seven in 1900 to seventy-four today) have come largely through saving our children by controlling childhood diseases so more persons have a chance to become older.

Another of the researchers, Dr. Breslau, said that every one of the health habits studied had a relationship to longevity and health. Men and women who were 10 percent under normal weight for their height had the highest death rate, suggesting that many of them may have had debilitating disease. Surprisingly, persons 5 to 19 percent overweight lived longest. The President's Council on Physical Fitness and Sports suggests that this may be due to the fact that most fit, well-muscled adults are overweight according to the standard weight charts.

Our eating habits are also very important. In many instances, persons who do not drink or smoke may have poor nutritional habits which are keeping them from attaining their physical best.

Overweight. In answering the question: "Does being heavy shorten life?" the Gerontology Research Center at the University of California analyzed the Baltimore Longevity Study for clues. In the Baltimore study a group of 650 healthy, well-educated men ranging in age from their early 20s to the late 90s were periodically examined with exhaustive mental and physical tests.

The study has gone on for 20 years and since 1978 women were added. Every scrap of data has been grist for the mill. The Baltimore study was supplemented by reports from different populations from all walks of life. Information from persons in Massachusetts, welfare recipients in Chicago, and citizens of England and Australia has been put together to provide a surprising conclusion about weight and aging. Dr. Rubin Andres, clinical director of the National Institutes of Health, after poring over every available report containing information on obesity and mortality rates, concluded, "The ideal weights as given on the commonly available height-weight tables are unrealistically below the levels desired—if what you are interested in is total mortality." People who were 20 to 30 percent over the chart weights did not in fact die any younger than those of normal weight. A few studies even showed that the moderately obese lived longer!

Dr. Andres, who is admittedly "chubby" himself, finds this exceedingly interesting. After all, obesity is a known risk factor in such killing diseases as hypertension and coronary artery disease. "Therefore," he says, "you would expect the total mortality to be higher for heavier people. But it isn't, and so it raises a question: Is there some sort of protective benefit in being obese that balances out these bad effects? Despite the other disadvantages of being fat—like not looking good in a bikini or prejudice against you in job hunting—you cannot truthfully say that someone who exceeds his desirable weight by 20 percent is shortening his life."
—Reported by Carol Kahn in "What Happens When We Get Old," *Family Health* (September 1979), p. 24

Caution: Let us not read too much into this report. We can easily eat too much and the wrong foods. We can get too heavy and carry an unnecessary burden. We shouldn't excuse ourselves, either, by rationalizing that our bodies are inherited and we can't do anything to alter our genetic endowments.

Marriage lengthens life. A study by the United States Department of Health, Education, and Welfare revealed: "Interestingly, older married people, compared to the same age-groups who are widowed, divorced, or have never married, live longer. This difference in age rate by marital status is not fully understood; it may reflect many complex factors—for example, the influence of poor health on the likelihood of marriage at all" (reported in *Health and the Later Years of Life,* 1971, p. 14).

Dental health

It is particularly important that younger and middle-aged persons understand the implications of poor dental hygiene and health care. Many younger people have unhealthy mouths which influence and deter them from developing a successful holistic approach to health.

Few younger persons realize the facial, emotional, physical, and nutritional consequences of poor dental hygiene which could come later in their lives such as:
1. **Poor nutrition as a result of inability to chew food properly. Also many times wrong foods are chosen because of the inability to chew properly.**
2. **Pain due to sore teeth or gums makes eating a torture rather than a pleasure.**
3. **Social embarrassment from poor teeth or no teeth causes some to isolate themselves.**
4. **Teeth are a part of good communication—a necessity for proper diction.**
5. **The loss of teeth without proper dentures distorts the facial appearance and produces a "hatchet-faced" profile.**
6. **Poor oral hygiene detracts from one's self-image.**

If the denture fits. For many years the American Dental Association has recognized that dental health care for older citizens is critical. The dental profession knows that the health care it renders is an essential part of a total health service. Following are some of the recommendations made to their members:

The need for dental care among the chronically ill and the aged who are residents of nursing homes is well recognized by the dental profession. If the needs of the chronically ill and the aged are to receive the attention they deserve, leadership by the health professions is essential.

The following statements and suggestions for dental care for the chronically ill and the aged are submitted:
1. **All nursing home residents should receive a dental examination at the time of their initial entrance into the home.**
2. **Local dental societies should develop programs to**

provide for relief of pain and elimination of infection for nursing home residents.

3. **Ambulatory residents should be transported to the dental office of their choice for necessary treatment.**
4. **Portable dental equipment should be available in order that dentists may render necessary treatment in the nursing home for non-ambulatory patients.**
5. **Some method of providing payment for care should be developed for those nursing home residents who desire care but who are not financially able to purchase it. The method should be determined at the community level.**

—The American Dental Association in a letter to its members (December 13, 1961)

A ways to go. Although these recommendations were made in 1961, conditions cited in the June 25, 1979, issue of *American Dental Association News* show that dental hygiene improvement among the elders has a long way to go. Mary Elizabeth Davies was reported to be greatly shocked when she toured a partially constructed geriatric care center at Pittston, Pennsylvania. She said, "They had a beauty parlor, false fireplace, but no dental facility. I was upset and angry. They told me no one ever mentioned dental care."

Robert E. Riddle, DDS, Goshen, Indiana, has had a lot of firsthand experience with this problem and finds it most frustrating. He comments in a letter (Jan. 28, 1980): "I believe a special room could be provided with very little additional expense to provide some basic services to nonambulatory patients in these institutions."

Few institutional homes make provision for a mobile dental unit facility. It is an issue most often kept far in the background. Generally, much can be learned about priorities by checking where the money is spent. Many administrators seem to take a dim view of dental care for their residents. The percentage spent for dental health care is declining.

Making the bite felt. Society, including older persons, has adopted the attitude that it may not be much use to do certain things for older persons because their time on earth is short and we do not think of them as persons with individual needs and personal gifts.

The condition of older persons in our society will improve only when they are no longer identified merely as a residue of life, but as persons who play a functional role in society. The critical importance of oral health maintenance must be made evident not only to the elderly, the administrators of homes, the dentists, but also to those who make health planning decisions on the local and national levels.

Mental health

"A mentally healthy person is one who has interest in work, family, friends, hobbies, and community activities," according to psychiatrists at the Menninger Foundation, Topeka, Kansas.

Dr. William Menninger, one of the foundation's founders, defines emotional maturity as:
1. **Having the ability to deal constructively with reality.**
2. **Having the ability to adapt to change.**
3. **Having relative freedom from symptoms that are produced by tensions and anxieties.**
4. **Having the capacity to find more satisfaction in giving than receiving.**
5. **Having the capacity to relate to other people in a consistent manner with mutual satisfaction and helpfulness.**
6. **Having the capacity to sublimate, to direct one's instinctive hostile energy into creative and constructive outlets.**

The development of a well-integrated personality can effect longevity. To develop well-integrated personalities we need healthy minds. Throughout our lives all of us come into situations which cause anxiety, stress, concern, fear, and tension. This is a fact of life and only the foolhardy would expect to find life otherwise.

From our earliest years we continue to shape our personalities in a manner which will determine whether or not we can cope with stresses with a degree of flexibility which will help us bend without breaking. The ability to manage life adequately is one which is built upon from day to day, cumulative in nature, and is never completed. All of us die undereducated about life management techniques. The development of a well-integrated personality can effect longevity.

Avoid mental illness. Good mental health implies that we are free from acute mental illness, that we can recognize the conditions which lead to mental disability and understand the factors which lead to mental deterioration. Also we must be able to identify the difference between organic and functional disease and learn to cope with conditions each might present to us.

All diseases can be placed in two classes: (1) organic diseases and (2) functional diseases. Organic diseases are those in which the mind or will of the patient has no part, either in the origin of the disease, or its cause thereafter. Functional diseases are caused by the mind or emotions of the patient. In the strictest sense, these diseases have no organic or anatomical basis. It is not always clear which diseases fall into which category.
—Jonathan G. Yoder, MD, in *Healing: Prayer or Pills?*(Herald Press, 1975), p. 34

Few persons have seen more physical and mental illness and under such diverse conditions than Dr. Yoder and his wife, Fyrne. For many years they were missionaries in India and Nepal, where Dr. Yoder performed thousands of operations and treated many traumatic mental conditions. He has also practiced broadly in the United States and continues after nearly fifty years as a medical doctor.

Develop flexible adaptive response to change. Dr. Francis J. Braskin retired at age sixty-five as director of the Institute of Living, Hartford, Connecticut. He retired "to avoid ending up ingloriously like biblical Jacob: leaning on his staff," he said and he chuckled. (Actually, Jacob (Gen. 41:37) was leaning on his bedstead when he bowed out.)

Dr. Braskin said, "Medicine kept us younger; stress and technology are making us older. The best way to stay youthful is to develop flexible adaptive responses to any changes. If not, we are prone to develop depression or psychosis." He further indicated that most of us have some difficulties emotionally, "but that should not make us anxious or paranoid. If not old age, our character and temperament determine our emotional health. To some, youth and age are equally a burden."

A reason for living is important. A reason for living is probably the most important element of successful living. A lifelong program of good mental health will increase both the quantity and quality of our days. Persons must learn the qualities which persons who have gone before them have found to permeate successful living—older persons who have learned to accentuate the positive.

Religion and mental health. Psychologist Donald T. Campbell of Northwestern University, one-time president of the American Psychological Association, was not timid in stating his views on religion to the American Psychological Association convention in Chicago in 1975.

Why is the president of the American Psychological Association saying nice things about original sin, confession of guilt, and the Ten Commandments? Why is he chiding his fellow psychologists for siding with self-gratification over self-restraint and for regarding guilt as a neurotic symptom? Because, after years of study and his avocational interest in evolutionary theory, he has finally come to believe that religion and other moral traditions are not only useful but scientifically valid.

"All the dominant modern psychologies," Campbell declared, "are individualistically hedonistic, explaining all human behavior in terms of individual pleasure and pain, individual needs and drives." They not only describe man as selfishly motivated, but "implicitly or explicitly teach that he ought to be so." Campbell called on psychologists to broaden "our narrowly individualistic focus" and to begin studying social systems with the assumption of "an underlying wisdom in the recipes for living that tradition has supplied us." They might, he said, be "better tested than the best of psychology's and psychiatry's speculations on how lives should be lived."

—From the article "Morals Make a Comeback" (Sept. 15, 1975), reprinted by permission from *Time*, The Weekly Newsmagazine; copyright Time Inc. 1975.

Holistic/wholistic health planning and living. The word "holistic" can be traced to the Greek word "holos" meaning whole, complete, and total. It emphasizes organic and functional relationships between parts and wholes.

"Wholistic" is a concept developed by Dr. Granger Westberg of Hinsdale, Illinois, which places a special emphasis on the spiritual dimension while also recognizing and including the physical, mental, and social aspects of wholeness. Westberg has become a national and even an international authority on spiritual counseling. The word "wholistic" is not now found in most dictionaries but in time it might well be. Westberg's concept has helped many to move from sickness care orientation to preventive health care orientation by recognizing all the components of good health, but particularly the spiritual, which many leaders in the health field do not recognize adequately.

Luke, the biblical physician, recognized the wholistic concept of healthful development when he recorded the growth of Jesus: "And Jesus increased in wisdom [mind], and stature [body], and in favor with God [spiritual] and man [community]" (Lk. 2:52).

Dr. Luke recognized wholeness also in recording the cleansing of the ten lepers (Lk. 17, KJV). Jesus healed the lepers, but nothing further is said about nine of them except that they were cleansed. The tenth leper, a Samaritan, who was also physically healed, went back to Jesus shouting praise to God. He bent low to express thanks and gratitude. Jesus told him, "Thy faith hath made thee whole."

There is a great difference between cleansing the body and being made whole. Seeking wholeness is not only a good health practice, but an unexcelled living style.

INVOLVEMENT: Living with centenarian Orpha Nusbaum

Alvin and Betty Nusbaum of Middlebury, Indiana, in 1974 made room in their home and their lives for then 99-year-old Orpha Nusbaum, Alvin's stepmother. It has worked because "Orpha is an easy person to get along with," Mrs. Nusbaum said. Orpha Ulrey Mishler Nusbaum has wide interests that keep her busy. She takes care of herself, although she eats breakfast and dinner with Mr. and Mrs. Nusbaum and their youngest daughter, Sara.

The town's celebrity citizen came to the Nusbaum home to convalesce after suffering a broken wrist in a fall in her own home. After the two-month convalescence, the elder Mrs. Nusbaum moved back to her own home two blocks away, but "she didn't care for it anymore," her stepson said. With the Nusbaums' invitation to return, Orpha, as she is known to her friends, said goodbye to her house, sold her things, and moved into the downstairs bedroom the couple made available to her. It seemed a natural move since the extended family had gotten along so well during the convalescence.

While the living arrangement has involved a good deal of give and take, it has been possible "because we take it a day at a time," Alvin Nusbaum said. He would recommend the arrangement only in rare circumstances, and then only with a single person. Orpha is that rare person. Alvin has been a school bus driver since 1942 and worked for many years at a local greenhouse and nursery. Mrs. Nusbaum works four hours a day in the cafeteria of the Middlebury elementary school. Their other daughter and son and their families live nearby, in the country.

The living arrangement has meant "getting family concerns clear sometimes," Betty Nusbaum said. "Orpha thought I didn't like her being here because I was never around to talk with her," daughter Sara said. "But I was just busy with sports, studies, and other things at school." The two have a mutual interest in Sara's cat, Friday. Betty commented, "Sure there are ups and downs, but I feel as though I'm doing something."

Orpha is a ready source of information, Alvin said. He sometimes asks her for clarification of a Scripture passage. Orpha served with her first husband in the free ministry in the Church of the Brethren. More often than not she will discover something new in the Scriptures she reads. She listens to religious services on Sunday morning and to some other favorite programs during the week. She continues to pursue her avocation of writing poetry, begun at about the age of ninety.

Mrs. Nusbaum picks up the mail on the way home from school each afternoon. Usually there is something for Orpha. At Christmas she received 75 cards, and for her birthday—105 on

August 13, 1979—she got more than 100 cards and letters. She answers each one individually. A few friends call regularly and she talks with others on the telephone. When she could get out she would call on up to 75 people a week.

Great-grandchildren are treated to candy and stories in Orpha's room. Not having had any children of her own, Orpha inherited almost twenty grandchildren when she married Frank Nusbaum in 1948. He died in 1959. Alvin is the youngest of four siblings. Orpha's first husband, John Mishler, died in 1941.

While the family was gone New Year's Day 1980, Orpha did something for the first time in her life. She turned on the TV to watch the Rose Bowl parade. She had watched the parade before, but had never turned on a TV. When she told of what she had done, Betty said, "Good! I'm glad you did!"

Orpha Nusbaum sometimes wonders why she has been left here, but since she is here she has to make the best of it, she says. A family which allows her independence and gives her the security she needs has made Orpha's latter years a stimulating period in her life and has given the family a sense that there "will be an empty spot when she's gone." At the time of this writing, she is still with us at age 107.

OUR BLESSINGS

You gave us a nose that we can smell,
And of the fragrance others tell.
A tongue to taste things that are good,
To pity those who have no food.
And eyes to see each other's needs,
For we were made to do good deeds.
And feet to walk the narrow way,
And knees that we can kneel and pray.
A voice to sing, a tongue to tell,
Glad tidings of Emmanuel.
And ears of course were made to hear,
And in your Book you've made it clear,
We are not here to take our ease,
We dare not do just as we please.
There's nothing, Lord, that we do lack,
Until we are flat on our back.
Oh! Then it's easy, Lord, to pray,
And this is what we'll likely say,
"Dear Lord, if you will make me well,

I will the blessed story tell."
But how much better it would be
If while we are well, we'd bow our knee
And sing your praises day by day
Until we're wafted far away.
—Orpha Nusbaum in her *Nuggets of Gold,*
given as a gift to her family and friends

STARTERS

1

Ponder the statement: "Life is a continuum from conception to inevitable physical death. Physiological and psychological changes, although inevitable, can become much more acceptable through understanding and education on the part of both the individual and society. Many pathological changes (structural and functional changes produced by disease) can be altered by better behavioral and health habits and by a better social and spiritual climate in the early and middle years." What are your parents' or grandparents' habits of healthful living? Sit down with them and discuss this chapter as it affects them and you.

2

Would you want to live past a hundred years? Don't accept an immediate "no" or a noncommital answer. Search out information on persons who have lived a century or more and share your findings with a person over sixty-five.

3

List three ways you are pleasing God. Test these marks of your pilgrimage with an older person who was a role model for you. Pay a compliment where compliment is due!

4

Thankful for pain? Church and other periodicals from time to time publish stories, poems, news of persons who, although made to suffer in illness or accident, find an overcoming spirit stronger than the condition or cure itself. Communicate a word of interest, comfort, appreciation to persons facing a health crisis—including their spouse, children, close friends.

5

As a member of a nursing home auxiliary, review the dental services provided to residents. Your next project might be to assist the administration in providing suitable facilities for dental care.

6

Watch your diet. Use recipes that call for basic ingredients (rather than highly processed foods). Share a meal each week or month with an older person who usually eats alone.

7

Continue the ongoing quest in search for self—the discovery and enhancement of the things which are most truly and profoundly you. As you come to understand the maturation process, you will avoid being overwhelmed physically, socially, emotionally, and spiritually as time moves on. Spend a few moments reflecting on the following specifics concerning aging:

a. At every stage in life you are determining the kind of person you will be later.

b. You always take yourself with you as you grow older—baggage and all.

c. How you live now is the most important factor in determining how you grow older.

d. You should understand the aging process before you become elderly.

e. Old age is not a crisis; aging is a law of life.

f. The future of younger persons will be longer than that of any previous generation.

g. What kind of person do you really want to be?

3 What Happens to Your Body Naturally

The human body, physical and mental, is the crown of God's creation. In the words of the psalmist, we are truly fearfully and wonderfully made. Yet we entertain fears about getting older. Understanding what happens to our bodies biologically can save us from anxiety and prepare us for compensating for physical limitations.

A decline begins in the efficiency of bodily functions at about age thirty and continues for the rest of our life. God has given us wisdom to cope with this change. When our eyes become dim, when our strength wanes, when strong men are bent and the sound of the grinding is low, the preacher in Ecclesiastes notes, it is not the end of living; rather, a law of creation is being fulfilled. We should understand this law of life and continue to give the best of what we have.

In Matthew 6:25 Christ shows the reciprocal relationship between physical aging and mental health. The mind has a goal above simply deciding what we should eat, what we should drink, or what we should wear. Undue emphasis on material things may lead to anxiety which can't add even a small measure to our life span—in fact, worry can shorten the life span. By exercising our mental faculties, the peak of God's creation, we are not only able to compensate for physical decline but are also given the potential to seek God and his righteousness above all else. "Therefore I tell you, do not be anxious about your life. . . . Is not life more than food, and the body more than clothing?"

(Mt. 6:25). We may approach the subject of biological aging—what happens to our bodies naturally—with anticipation, not fear.

Aging defined

Aging is the sum total of the adverse physical, sociological, and mental changes that take place within us which are not attributable to illness or disease. It is a term used to describe the processes of biological, psychological, and sociological change from one point of time to another. Aging is not a youth deficiency. However, society has yet to fully outgrow the Roman attitude, *senectus ipsa morbus* (old age is in itself a disease).

Aristotle (384-322 B.C.) said that old age is not a disease because it is not contrary to nature. Many older persons—particularly the socially isolated, including the minorities, the financially disadvantaged, and those in poor health—do suffer the civil wounds inflicted by time and also the spiritual wounds dealt them by society and too often by the church. This is not normal aging. As more persons are discovering the potential of rewarding older years, more younger persons are changing their attitudes. They are seeing their own potential for aging and for helping others find rewarding older years.

Act your age: How old are you?

It is difficult to determine our respective ages since the maturation process is a composite of many facets. Our chronological age may be the least significant facet. LeRoy (Satchel) Paige, one of the first black major league baseball players, had been kept out of professional baseball because of his color until age forty-two. He was a winning pitcher for four years. When asked his age, he would answer: "How old would you be if you did not know how old you were?"

A philosopher as well as a player, Paige recognized the relative significance of number of years. The sum of how old we are becomes intelligible only as we include other factors. Consider the jingle about Father William:

**You are old, Father William, the young man said,
And your hair has become very white.**

**Yet you increasingly stand on your head.
Do you think at your age this is right?**

If Father William likes to stand on his head, if it does not deter him from standing on his feet, if he doesn't become a public nuisance, or if too many people aren't offended, is it wrong?

Young and old are imprecise terms. One person may be an "old" PhD at thirty-two and a "young" professor thirty years later. Another may be a "young" PhD candidate at twenty-five and an "old" professor five years later. We must guard against letting inappropriate notions about advancing years keep us from experiencing the life-rounding process of maturing in all the ways we grow older.

Seven ages

A composite age classification may include the following categories:

1. **Chronological.** The date of our physical birth.

2. **Physical-biological.** No two persons are alike biologically, and the rate of change is different for various parts of the body in the same person.

3. **Psychological-mental.** Changes and degrees of change in sensory function, perception, memory, learning, intelligence, and the dynamics of personality affect alertness, proficiency, ability to handle stress, and ability to learn.

4. **Social.** Other considerations include the degree of social maturity and awareness, the response the individual makes to social stimuli, and the ability to adapt to the changing conditions of time, space, and physical, economic, and psychological factors. Attitudes of society are involved. "Old" means different things in different cultures.

5. **Legal.** When is one responsible for certain acts? When are we "of age"? When do we have certain "rights"? For how long? Voting, attending school, driving a car, retirement?

6. Age of accountability. This is the time at which we become accountable for certain spiritual or religious decisions. Do we want to join a religious body or congregation? Which one? What code of ethics do we want to follow?

7. Functional or competency. What have we done? What are we doing now? What are we capable of doing? What do we want to do? How well can we cope?

Definitions

Biologically, life is a continuum without radical segmentation. One part of life is just as important as another. There are continuous changes but no sharp natural gradations as life moves on in its uninterrupted sequence. Biological aging in a broad sense is the sum total of the changes which take place in an individual's life from conception to the last breath of physical life—changes in bodily functions which are attributable to natural causes and not to accident or disease. These adverse changes accumulate and decrease the ability of the body to function and finally culminate in physical death.

Growth and atrophy are simultaneous

Aging in Today's Society describes simultaneous growth and atrophy thus:

Aging involves two simultaneous processes which operate continuously in spite of the fact that they are contradictory to one another. On the one hand growth or evolution occurs; on the other, atrophy (which means shrinkage) or involution. These processes continue throughout life, though at varying rates. We can observe illustrations of atrophy even before the infant is born in the disappearance of the gill clefts which first develop and then atrophy in the early mammalian embryo.

At the time of birth, when the child begins to breathe and get its oxygen from the lungs instead of from the mother's circulation, the atrophy of certain arterial structure is indistinguishable under the microscope from the involuntary changes which we see late in life. The atrophic process is the same in the newborn infant and in the senile grandparent. A very interesting phenomenon occurs in the placenta or afterbirth. It becomes atrophic or "old" when

its functional life is near termination. At nine months of
pregnancy, these exist in intimate proximity and interde-
pendence in a very young baby, a middle-aged mother,
and a senile placenta. Biologically adjacent and functioning together are three widely divergent biological ages.
Here is an area of study which has by no means been explored adequately.
—Clark Tibbits and Wilma Donahue, editors, *Aging in Today's
Society*, p. 45

Our biological time clocks are set individually

Our biological time clocks are set to completely individual
circumstances; no two persons can be compared in rate of
change either in development or in our maximum physical
strengths or in our losses. In addition, the degenerative process
may be evident in some body organs while other functions in the
same body become stronger.

At about thirty years of age, the time that is ironically
called the prime of life, the degenerative process starts
and man starts to deplete the reserve capacity that has
been established in his youth. However, the rest of man's
life is adaptive in the sense that his body compensates
physiologically for the decrease in reserve.
—Adeline M. Hoffman, editor, in *The Daily Needs and
Interests of Older People* (C. C. Thomas, 1970), p. 195

Dr. Thomas K. Cureton, professor of physical education
and director of the Physical Fitness Research Laboratory at the
University of Illinois, tested 50,000 men and women over a period of 33 years. He found that the peak of physical fitness comes
on the average at twenty-six years of age.

Physiological aging is the gradual loss of physical
powers and capacities after gradual build-up to 17, the plateau extending from 17 to 26, and the decline beginning at
an average of about 26 years of age. We define "middle
age" as the 26 to 65 age span during which there is a
steady loss of various powers and abilities. This is
followed by the gerontological (66+) old-age range, now of
accelerated interest to gerontology and specifically to
geriatrics medicine. However, research indicates that
chronological age is a poor classifier and actual functional

fitness tests are better to indicate the degree of integration between the mind and the body—i.e., the capacity to work and the distance away from schizophrenia.
—*Australian Journal of Physical Education,* No. 32, November 1964

Ms. Simone De Beauvoir, a French gerontologist (one of the world's most renowned), indicates some of the physical functions which maximize early in life and then slowly diminish:

1. **The margin of visual accommodation diminishes from the age of ten (note the number of children who wear glasses or contact lenses).**
2. **Before adolescence the hearing of very high sounds diminishes.**
3. **Unstructured memory grows weaker after twelve.**
4. **Sexual potency in men declines after sixteen.**
5. **Between twenty and thirty a retrograde alteration in the organs begins.**
   —Simone De Beauvoir in *The Coming of Age* (Warner Books), p. 12

Slow decline after thirty

Depending on the type of activity, the highest physical performance may be reached at a very early chronological age. Many of the world's records in swimming are held by young teenagers. Chris Evert, the outstanding woman athlete of 1974, was the Wimbledon winner; she was also considered the world's champion in tennis at age nineteen. But Evert was beaten by sixteen-year-old Tracy Austin in 1979. Jimmy Connors was the men's Wimbledon champion in 1974 at age twenty-one. His opponent in the finals was Ken Rosewald, nearly twice Connors' age.

Older persons can do quite well competitively into later years in some areas. Sam Snead tied for second place in the Los Angeles Open gold championship in December 1973, when he was nearly sixty-two. In golf you can take your time. Persons even vaguely familiar with distance-running competition are aware of the ability of distance runners to improve with age and to attain their greatest success in their late twenties or early thirties. It is not unusual to observe men competing in long-

distance runs at the age of fifty years. A classic example was
Clarence DeMar, "Mr. DeMar-athon," who won his seventh
Boston Marathon at the age of forty-two years, placed seventh at
the age of fifty years, and finished seventy-eighth in a field of 133
runners at the age of sixty-five.

Although older persons can continue to perform well in
many different kinds of sports and other recreational activity,
they should expect to get real satisfaction and benefit from doing
what can be reasonably expected rather than from expecting to
win championships.

God provided adequate reserves

Seldom is anyone called upon to produce at the maximum.
God, who created each of us as special individuals, in his infinite
wisdom gave us ample reserves to perform the tasks we are called
upon to perform at a given time. He also gave us minds to
develop eye-glasses, hearing aids, transportation, elevators, and
labor-saving devices. Helpful and compassionate persons make
life easier. A hierarchy of labor expectations allows older persons
to receive a reasonable share of society's benefits without
maximum physical exertions.

Etienne, the French philosopher, said hundreds of years ago
that "God tempers the wind to the shorn lamb." The church and
the community do well to temper their minds to seek out older
citizens and minister to them.

Much can be learned from the ancient Confucius, 500 BC,
who lived to be seventy-two, more than twice the life expectancy
for his time. He might have been the first theorist in age stratifi-
cation. His theory of human development did not see the last
part of life as inevitable senility, but as a part of a continuum.
Indeed, old age to him was life in the highest form: "At fifteen I
applied myself to the study of wisdom, at thirty I grew stronger
in it, at forty I no longer have doubt, at fifty there is nothing on
earth that would shake me, and at seventy I could follow the
dictate of my heart without disobeying moral laws."

Physical signs of biological aging

1. The senses become less sharp. Diseases, repeated injuries,
continued loud noise levels, and excessive physical, mental, or

emotional demands account for some losses, but age itself accounts for a good deal of loss.

1. Vision tends to become less sharp after adolescence. A fifty-year-old needs twice as much light to read than at twenty. An eighty-year-old needs three times as much light. Diffused light is needed and not sharp contrasts because older eyes are more sensitive to glare.
2. Hearing losses begin at twenty and continue throughout life, particularly in the higher frequencies. The inability to hear the higher pitches can go unnoticed but the older person is apt to think that "everyone mumbles." Beginning about fifty-five, men's hearing losses are greater than women's. Older persons are more apt to appreciate the rich low tones of organ music than the current music youngsters enjoy. Doorbells, telephones, and voices should all be low-toned.
3. Taste buds are reduced to 45 percent at seventy. Older persons need spicier foods. Tart rather than sweet foods are preferred generally. (Don't complain because your wife's cooking doesn't taste like it used to!)
4. The sense of touch is reduced.
5. It is more difficult to keep one's balance.
6. The sense of smell does not change much but there are losses by some.
—Adapted from James D. Manney, Jr., in *Aging in Modern Society*, University of Michigan Press, Ann Arbor, 1975

2. There is a general slowing down of certain types of responses. Simone De Beauvoir outlined some of the biological signs of aging as follows:

1. Motor skills lessen.
2. Decreasing ability to respond quickly to complex activities and unfamiliar demands.
3. Graying or loss of hair. Hair may appear in new places, i.e., chins and lips of women.
4. Skin becomes thinner and brown blotches appear.
5. Skin may become wrinkled (called character lines by older persons).
6. Body becomes less sensitive to extreme heat and cold (parts can freeze or burn with only limited awareness).
7. Body becomes shorter (one to two inches) through compression of spinal discs and vertebrae.
8. Body may become stooped (it helps to walk "tall" and sit "tall").

9. **Teeth may become diseased and come out (there are nearly 30,000,000 toothless adults in United States).**
10. **Particularly with loss of teeth but often unrelated, the nose and chin become closer together (the nose lengthens and the upper lip becomes thinner comparatively).**
11. **Ear lobes are apt to increase in relative length.**
12. **The skeleton may suffer from osteoporosis, meaning that the dense part of such bones as the femur may become porous and fragile, leading to easy fractures.**
    —Adapted from Simone De Beauvoir in *The Coming of Age* (Warner Books), p. 12

Comparative physiological losses

From studies done at the gerontology branch of the National Institutes of Health, at Baltimore City Hospital in Baltimore, Maryland, the physiological decline which accompanies aging was plotted. The chart below gives the approximate percentages of functions or tissues remaining to the average seventy-year-old person, taking the value found for the average thirty-year-old as 100 percent:

1.	**Maximum work rate**	70%
2.	**Maximum work rate in short spurts**	15%
3.	**Basal metabolic rate—building up protoplasm**	84%
4.	**Body weight**	88%
5.	**Brain weight**	56%
6.	**Recent memory loss**	50%
7.	**Slower speed of response**	50%
8.	**Blood flow to brain**	80%
9.	**Number of taste buds**	36%
10.	**Maximum breathing capacity (voluntary)**	43%
11.	**Vital capacity (exchange of air in and out of lungs)**	56%
12.	**Muscle strength (hand grip)**	55%
13.	**Ability of kidneys to remove waste**	56%
14.	**Homeostasis—ability of body to restore equilibrium or normal state once it is disturbed**	17%

—Adeline M. Hoffman in *The Daily Needs and Interests of Older People* (C. C. Thomas, 1976), p. 197

No one should take these statistics too literally or too personally. Some individuals function better at seventy than others do at thirty. Too many people fail to function at a reasonable capacity solely because they think they are old. Many capable individuals are satisfied to retire to their rockers long before they need to and, unfortunately, prolonged failure to use tissue results in wasting and atrophy. Thus, muscles become weak and bones fragile, which further limits the physical activity of sedentary older people.

Losses should be expected and accepted

Older persons suffer many losses which should be expected and accepted. The really important solutions will not come from brooding over our losses but in appraising what we have, coping with limitations, and using remaining resources in a creative beneficial way. Proper diet and regular exercise are two factors that can mitigate the effects of aging. What are we doing with what we have?

INVOLVEMENT: Trimming the toenails

As nurse on call at Greencroft, a retirement community and nursing home in Goshen, Indiana, Kathryn Leatherman works with people who must step into new shoes. These people must adjust to the biological changes of old age—changes involving tissues, bowels, appetite, and vitamins, to name but a few.

Such physical alterations are often difficult to accept; they put the older person in the unfamiliar role of dependency. Kathryn mentioned foot care as one example: "A lot of people find it embarrassing to have someone else trim their toenails. I try to help them understand that their situation is not unique, that as they grow older, many folks can't reach their feet anymore."

Kathryn believes that it is only after older persons have recognized their physical limitations that they can compensate for them and thus avoid the nursing home. For instance, she has helped those with failing memories to understand the necessity for listing their problems in black and white before visiting the doctor who may ask what's wrong and then zip out before the older person can remember. For residents with heart conditions, poor appetites, or fragile bones, Kathryn says that compensation through exercise, diet, and the right equipment (such as walkers and elevating commodes) has spelled the difference between nursing home and independent housing. To prepare for the biological changes of old age and to prevent stress from occurring, Kathryn has special advice for women, whom she encourages to develop a better idea of how to take care of themselves. The majority of residents at Greencroft are women, Kathryn observes, "and some of them have had a satin pillow all their lives—first their parents and then their husbands."

Kathryn tells about one eighty-five-year-old resident who was on her own for the first time. When the doctor told her to take a certain medication for dizziness, the woman asked Kathryn, "How do I decide when I'm dizzy?"

As preparation for old age, Kathryn also advises younger people of both sexes to follow good health practices and to develop a variety of hobbies. She once knew a man who loved wood carving but then became allergic to the wood as he grew older. "Because he didn't have any other hobbies, all he'd do was sit around."

Kathryn believes that by middle age a person should be considering his view of life and death. "I don't think I've heard any of the residents here express the fear of dying," she said. "But they often tell me they fear ending up helpless, in a nursing home, with their physiological processes kept going through artificial means. When they share this fear, I tell them it's their responsibility to talk with their doctor about the extent of the measures they expect him to take to sustain life."

In these and other ways, Kathryn Leatherman is helping residents at Greencroft to adjust to the wide range of biological changes which occur with old age. Whenever old feet must put on new shoes, Kathryn cares enough to make sure they fit.

STARTERS

1

Ponder your worth: "Lord, I am fearfully and wonderfully made." What does the following have to say about how you live?

In 1900 two persons out of ten died of tuberculosis. Today TB deaths represent a small fraction of one percent. Diphtheria took one out of ten in 1900, but today is scarcely a factor. In 1979 smallpox was declared extinct. New drugs, vaccines, and advanced medical skills and technology have tremendously influenced longevity. Life expectancy in the United States has reached seventy-seven years for women and sixty-nine years for men.

Today 11 percent, or 25,000,000 persons, are sixty-five and over in the USA. In 1900 it was 4 percent. Canadian figures are comparable. Increased longevity has been realized principally by saving children. In 1800 about 50 percent of children died before age ten; today only a small percent die before ten. Eighty percent of infants born alive today are expected to reach age sixty-five. In 1900, 80 percent did not.

If we were able to control the ravages of cancer, strokes, and cardiovascular diseases we could add seven or eight years to the average life span. We would then be reaching the maximum suggested in Psalm 90:10: "The years of our life are threescore and ten, or even by reason of strength fourscore."

2

Proper diet and regular exercise are two factors at the individual's control which can lessen the effects of aging. What are your community, church, and family doing to meet this basic need of older persons?

3

Mental facility lies at the command of most persons. Guard against doing all the thinking for your parent or partner. Practice the art of "walking with" rather than always "doing for" an older person. Practice!

4

The idea of aging makes you anxious or fretful? Talk over your concerns with a former teacher or trusted older acquaintance. Open yourself to the life and wisdom of their years.

5

Arrange for a doctor or nurse to address an intergenerational group on the subject of biological changes. They may have some ideas of audio-visuals to use. The meeting could be held in the activities room, chapel, or dining room of an area retirement or nursing home.

6

How do you view the last days and hours of your life? Check your thoughts with the ideas in the chapter "Dying and Death."

7

What are you doing that builds maturity into your years? What changes should you make to avoid the negative forces of immaturity? Put your goals for one year on paper and check on your progress periodically. You may be surprised at what happens to you—naturally.

4 Beyond Tiddledywinks: Exercise and Humor

Not all are physical activists. Some sit and frown. Some lie down to think about it. One vacationer said, "I jog all the way to the pool." Some professional humorists may themselves not be happy persons. Yet both exercise and humor hold keys to fitness and a larger sense of wholeness and well-being. Both thrive on a right attitude. Both add fullness to our years.

How not to do it

The chief exercise for too many people has been carried out in such uncreative ways as running down their peers, wrestling with others' problems, casting aspersions, skipping responsibility, kicking about the way things are, throwing mud, jumping to conclusions, and resting on other people's laurels. These physical unfitness forms are not highly recommended for everyday or even occasional use. They do not become more meritorious through regular practice. They can't be done in good company.

Exercise yesterday and today

The current fitness kick is a far cry from the prevailing attitude of forty and more years ago expressed by Robert Hutchins, then president of the University of Chicago. Hutchins seemed to have caught the mood of his time with regard to exercise when he said, "When I feel like exercising I lie down and take a rest." Much earlier, Mark Twain (1835-1910) prescribed his secret for retaining his youth. Twain reported that once on a holiday in the Adirondacks he made a concerted effort to acquire enough exercise to last him the rest of his life. Writing to a friend he said, "I shall exert myself in everyway to harden my muscles and toughen and strengthen my frame. I shall use method in my exercises, too. I shall not lie under one tree until injury from overexertion sets in but changing to another now and then. And I shall not sit around until overheated but will watch my pulse and go to bed as soon as I am crowding my powers."

It is easy to observe the increase in athletic activity today. In nearly every community people of many ages are involved in various kinds of exercise. Forty years ago men and women would have been embarrassed to be seen jogging along the streets. Men would have been considered odd and women even odder. Today exercise is a fact of life.

Millions of Americans in the largest number ever are turning to strenuous exercises as an escape from illness, fatigue, and boredom of today's sedentary way of life. Behind all this interest in exercise is a growing awareness of the deteriorating physical conditions of most Americans.
—From "Why Sixty Million Americans Are on a Fitness Kick" in *U.S. News and World Report* (January 14, 1974)

Younger Americans are larger

In spite of the many shoddy health practices of today, Americans are healthier, live longer, and grow taller and heavier than ever before. Most of the supporting statistics are from army records which until recently did not include women. According to national health statistics 200 years ago the average American soldier was 5' 6" tall and weighed 130 pounds. Civil war veterans were approximately the same size. The typical eighteen-year-old male today weighs 150 pounds and is slightly more than 5' 9" in height. The typical eighteen-year-old female today is 5' 4½" tall, and weights 123 pounds. The increased size can be attributed to improved diet, better medical care, and the eradication of most childhood diseases which years ago stunted the growth of many children. It is possible, however, that we have reached our genetic potential since body size and weight have not changed significantly for approximately fifteen years.

Americans are wider astern than their ancestors

This increase in size of the average American is not without its problems and has exacted a price. For instance, the American Seating Company, the largest manufacturer of auditorium seating in the United States, interviewed 7,710 men and women between the ages of eighteen and seventy-nine. As a result of their findings the company added two inches to the width of its auditorium seats.

Exercises may or may not be appropriate

Exercise is important for most Americans, male and female, regardless of age. However, the types and forms appropriate to specific individuals should be determined with the advice of a physician. Thomas J. Cureton, formerly director of the Physical Fitness Laboratory of the University of Illinois, tested 50,000 men and women and helped several thousand recondition themselves. In a news report in early 1977 he said, "Health, endurance, nutrition, and general well-being are all dependent on a common denominator—circulatory fitness. The only way to get it is via a systematic method of exercise.

"As a man or woman gets older, youth gradually disappears in proportion to the ebbing of the metabolism and circulation," Cureton said. "To retain the physical capacities of youth, a person must maintain circulatory and muscular fitness. The fight is mainly to keep the capillaries open by constantly working the body. Otherwise, one will grow old prematurely."

Precautions

Exercises and sports properly directed, oriented, and supervised can be a boon to healthful living. Unsupervised and improperly implemented physical activity can be a complete "bust."

In 1977, 20,000,000 Americans were hurt in recreational athletics. (The figure was 12,000,000 in 1963 and 17,000,000 in 1971.) In hundreds of hospital emergency wards and physicians' waiting rooms they sit, these weekend warriors, with their tennis elbows; stress fractures; broken noses; tendinitis; dislocated shoulders,

**hips, and fingers; strains and sprains, not to mention
sundry bruises, abrasions, lacerations, and concussions.
The vast majority of injuries result from what doctors call
the "over-use syndrome," trying to push the out-of-condi-
tion over-thirty body too far too fast.
    Regular exercise can help make one healthier. The
injuries result from the delusion that a few hours of sports
are healthful. Eighty percent of the troubles could be
avoided, doctors point out, with some simple precautions.
According to Dr. Dinesh Patel, codirector of Massachusetts General Hospital Sports Medicine Clinic, 60
percent of athletic injuries could be prevented by training
and warm-up, another 20 percent by proper shoes and
prescreening. In selecting a sport, weight, body build, and
general flexibility must be considered. Fat people should
forsake jogging in favor of sports like swimming that mitigate the effects of gravity. No matter what the sport, it
should be worked into gradually with a warm-up of slow
stretches preceding activity, and if the body hurts, don't go
on.**
    —*Time* Magazine (August 21, 1978)

The most beneficial activities

    Many experts in physical exercise believe that the most
beneficial activities are walking, jogging, cycling, and swimming—depending upon what your physician recommends. Dr.
Robert Stamp, physician and health professor at the University
of Wisconsin at Madison, spent nineteen years studying why
some people live longer than others. He studied two groups:
those from seventy-five to 108 and those from fifty-four to
seventy. He found that few persons reach eighty years of age
without a routine of work or physical activity and that few older
people continue to live if the activity program which helped them
reach eighty is stopped by a disease, accident, or just wearing out.

The joys of walking

    Universally, walking can be one of the most practical and
beneficial forms of exercise. The late Paul Dudley White,
renowned heart specialist, said, "No one should use a golf cart
but by prescription."
    To get the most out of walking we must move rapidly if we

are able to do so. We should walk as though we "were going somewhere."

Some of the benefits of walking are:
1. Physical enjoyment of stretching the muscles.
2. Expanding lungs in rhythmic relaxation.
3. Aesthetic and adventuresome pleasure of finding and seeking new things.
4. Psychological advantage in getting away from the desk, the automobile, shopping lists, the sheer "dailiness" of daily life.
5. Walking is a heart saver. Our bodies are built for use.
6. Walking is a non-dieting diet. Overweight is an invitation to trouble.
7. Walking is antidote to tension. Even a short, fast walk can drain away anger and anxiety.
8. Walking requires no special facilities or equipment. A comfortable pair of shoes is all that is needed plus some simple walking clothes. During inclement weather some heart patients go to shopping malls to walk inside.
9. Walking demands no special time or place. Almost anyone can find walking space at the front door.

— *The Magic of Walking,* copyright 1967 by Aaron Sussman and Ruth Good. Reprinted by permission of Simon & Schuster, a division of Gulf & Western Corporation

---

The "perfect massage"

Walking is certainly not a new form of exercise. What may be new is that so many people walk by choice rather than from necessity. In 1926, just before his death at age ninety, Edward Payson Weston wrote that walking is like a perfect massage. It relaxes the muscles but unlike a massage, it also strengthens them. Weston, a reporter for the *New York Herald,* in 1861 decided to walk from Boston to Washington in ten days, in time for Lincoln's inauguration. He missed the ceremony by a half day but his effort caught the public's fancy. From that time on he set walking record after walking record in both distance and time. In 1909 he left New York for San Francisco and completed the hike in 105 days. Before his death on May 12, 1929, he walked thousands of miles in record time.

Calorie counter

Frequently people who exercise want to know the comparative calorie output from various forms of exercise. Here is one such listing:

	Calorie output per week
Walking at a brisk pace, three hours weekly	1200
Push-ups, half hour weekly	770
Golf, eighteen holes, three times weekly	1800
Gardening, five hours weekly	1500
Swimming, three hours weekly	1500
Cycling, four hours weekly	1250
Tennis, six hours weekly	1250
Volleyball, six hours weekly	1500
Bowling, five hours weekly	800

	Calorie output per hour
Walking moderately	200
Walking briskly	400
Running	800
Cycling	400
Swimming	500
Light exercise	85
Active exercise	205
Gardening	300

—Sussman and Good, *op. cit.*

Exercising the sixth sense: humor

In order that our days may be both long and fruitful on this earth we should have a sense of humor. Nearly all longevity studies have found this to be an important ingredient. It's difficult to survive the stresses of life unless we have social and spiritual equilibrium. Our daily walk should be earnest but joyous. We can't be at our best if our spirits droop and our emotional life is warped. A good sense of humor can become an important balance wheel.

To have a sense of humor does not mean that we become trite, fickle, silly, or irresponsible. It means rather that we do not take ourselves too seriously, our personal dignity can stand some adjusting, and we can actually learn to enjoy a situation where "the joke is on us." Humor can relieve tensions and keep us from becoming too rigid, too inflexible, lonely, suspicious, and fearful. Good humor may be a tonic for the soul, a release from tension, a balm in Gilead. "A cheerful heart is a good medicine, but a downcast spirit dries up the bones" (Prov. 17:22).

What is humor or wit?

The terms *humor* and *wit* are closely related. They suggest the ability both to express and perceive the subtle and un-predictable, the absurd and incongruous, the clever and amusing in special situations or occasions. Englist poet Alexander Pope (1688-1741) said, "True wit is to nature's advantage dressed; what oft was thought, but ne'er so well expressed." Not all at-tempts at wit or humor strike the same response in individuals or groups—some never strike at all!

Situations and timing are important, as illustrated in the story of six men in a retirement home who regularly gathered to tell stories. They became weary of repeating so many words before the punch line so they finally numbered their stories and would call out the number of their favorite one. Uproarious laughter followed. A newcomer joined the group one day and studied the process. He, too, finally called out a number. There was no response. Inquiring why his joke fell flat, he was told, "It depends how you tell it."

A second person or persons need not be involved. Humor depends on the emotional climate, a mood, an attitude, a recognition of our own humanity and our error-proneness. True humor is never sarcastic, haughty, arrogant, vulgar, boastful, or rude. Like love it is patient and kind and does not rejoice in wrong or in downgrading others, especially the unfortunate.

Not everyone is an expert in quick witty replies, nor in re-membering jokes, nor in telling jokes well, but nearly everyone can enjoy humorous situations. The Bible includes some good humor. It describes of the habitually lazy person this way: "The sluggard buries his hand in the dish; it wears him out to bring it back to his mouth" (Prov. 26:15). Leviticus (26:36, 37a) describes faintness of heart thus: "And as for those of you that are left, I will send faintness into their hearts in the lands of their enemies; the sound of a driven leaf shall put them to flight, and they shall flee as one flees from the sword, and they shall fall when none pursues. They shall stumble over one another, as if to escape a sword, though none pursues."

Poking fun at ourselves

Older persons are often the butt of unfavorable jokes which help perpetuate an unfavorable image of the aging process. At times older persons aid this process. An elderly man was sitting in the barber's chair and the barber asked him, "How are you today?" "Pretty good, pretty good," he replied. "They tell me I'm losing my mind but that doesn't bother me. I never used it much anyhow."

Recognizing our own humanity and our limitations by poking fun at ourselves once in awhile may be healthy, but we shouldn't make it a habit. The public doesn't need much encouragement in this area.

I have good news for you. The first eighty years are the hardest.

The second eighty, as far as my experience goes, is a succession of birthday parties. Everybody wants to carry your baggage and help you up the steps. If you forget anybody's name or forget to fulfill an appointment or promise ... you can explain that you are eighty. If you spill your soup on your necktie or fail to shave one side of your face or if your shoes don't match or you take another man's hat by mistake or carry a letter around in your pocket a week before you read it, you are eighty. So you can relax with no misgivings, for you have a perfect alibi for everything.

Nobody expects much of you. If you act silly it is your second childhood. Everybody is looking for symptoms of softening of the brain. Being eighty is a great deal better than being sixty-five or seventy. At that time they expect you to retire to a little house in Florida and become a discontented, grumbling, lisping has-been. But if you survive until eighty, everybody is surprised that you can talk above a whisper, surprised if you reveal signs of lucid intervals. At seventy, people are mad at you for everything; at eighty, they forgive anything. If you ask me, life begins at eighty!

—Frank C. Laubach

Laubach is not to be taken too literally, but he was recognizing in a humorous way the inner feeling of condescension some younger person may actually feel toward older persons.

An analysis of jokes about aging and death

In a February 1978 article in *Gerontologist* Timothy Weber and Paul Cemeron analyzed some previous articles in the same magazine which carried jokes about aging and death. Their purpose was to determine social attitudes toward this portion of the life span. Of 363 jokes about older persons, 63 percent were classified as negative and 22 percent ambivalent. This meant that only 15 percent were positive. In a second sample of jokes about death, 57 percent were negative, 18 percent ambivalent, and 25 percent positive. Certainly "jokes" and "humor" are not synonymous but the analysis does show us much about American attitudes toward older persons and death.

Laughter

We can enjoy humorous situations without laughing and we can laugh raucously about something which may scarcely be comical. However, a good belly laugh can benefit our body systems.

Scientists have been studying the effect of laughter on humans and have found, among other things, that laughter has a profound and instantaneous effect on virtually every important organ in the human body. Laughter reduces health-sapping tensions and relaxes the tissues, as well as exercising the most vital organs. It is said that laughter, even when forced, results in a beneficial effect on us, both mentally and physically.
—Author Unknown

Professional humorists who work for "laughs" are not necessarily happy persons. Many persons who carry an outwardly happy profile may be attempting to cover up an unhappy life. Other persons with inexpressive or even dour faces may, deep within, be happy well-adjusted persons.

They didn't know how to blush

From what we see on TV and from what we read and hear it seems almost anything goes these days. We have lost our sense of shock and shame. Blushing is a lost art. Unfortunately, many persons have allowed vulgarity to enter their speech and actions in their attempts to create humorous situations. Even in the times of Jeremiah, the biblical prophet, this was a problem (8:12a): "Were they ashamed when they committed abomination? No. They were not at all ashamed; they did not know how to blush." Good humor shouldn't cause anyone to blush—even those to whom it is not a lost art!

Humor through identification: Grandma's recipe

Here is an authentic washday "receipt" in its original spelling as it was written out for a bride four generations ago:

To do the wash:
1. Bild a fire in back yard to heet kettle of rain water.
2. Set tubs so smoke won't blow in eyes if wind is pert.
3. Shave one hole cake lie soap in bilin water.
4. Sort things, make three piles. 1 pile white. 1 pile cullord. 1 pile work britches and rags.
5. Stur flour in cold water to smooth, then thin down with bilin water.
6. Rub dirty spots on board, scrub hard, then bile—just rench and starch.
7. Take white things out of kettle with broom stick handle, then rench, blew, and starch.
8. Spred tee towels on grass.
9. Hang old rags on fence.
10. Pore rench water on flower bed.
11. Scrub porch with hot soapy water.
12. Turn tubs upside down.
13. Go put on cleen dress—smooth hair with side combs— brew cup of tea—set and rest and rock a spell and count blessings.

—Author Unknown

Speaking the truth in love

The presiding bishop, not known as a great speaker, visited one of the congregations in his district and was greeted by a small audience. The bishop was somewhat chagrined and asked the chairman of the board of elders if he had told the congregation of his visit. The chairman of the board responded: "No, I never said a word; they must have found it out some other way."

Too busy at the office

Thomas, a six-year-old boy, went to Sunday school for the first time with his friend Joel. He was impressed by the teacher's description of the beauties of heaven. On the way home Thomas said to Joel: "I've decided that I am going to heaven and I'll ask mother and sister to go along. I don't think I'll say anything to dad about it because he will be too busy at the office."

Wasting its fragrance

This story appeared in a service club magazine:

While traveling along one of the side roads in the Ozarks last fall my wife and I stopped at a mountaineer's cabin for directions. Not knowing quite how to begin, I said to the proprietor on the porch: "It must be kind of lonesome around here."

Before the toothless patriarch responded he looked me straight in the eye, unloaded a guided missile of nicotine, shifted his corncob pipe, and said: "Solitude is a state of mind which effectuates its reactionary tendencies and innoculates those with hypersensitivity. However, having been a victim of claustrophobia, in the environment of nature's wonders, not only do I find them serene and serious, but fundamentally mandatory."

We left in silence. A half mile down the trail my wife recovered her sense of verbal articulation, not often lost, and said: "Why didn't you say something, you dumb cluck?"

The next day a verse from Gray's "Elegy in a Country Church Yard" came to mind:

Full many a gem of purest ray serene,
    The dark unfathomed caves of ocean bear.
Full many a rose was born to blush unseen
    And waste its sweetness on the desert air.

Funerals

A mountaineer died after a life of fighting, drunkenness, feuding, and total disregard for his wife and family. At the funeral service the local preacher waxed eloquent in extolling the virtues of the deceased, emphasizing his exemplary life, his devotion to his family, and his peaceful demeanor. Finally the wife of the deceased became greatly perturbed and whispered to her daughter at her side: "Callie, you'd better go up and lift that lid; we must be at the wrong funeral."

The nut is gone

In the little country church in Ozark acorn country the preacher looked at the wooden casket before him and solemnly intoned before the family and friends assembled, in a figure of speech well understood: "All we have before us is the shell; the nut is gone."

Insights

Lord, thou knowest better than I know myself that I am growing older, and will some day be old.

Keep me from getting talkative, and particularly from the fatal habit of thinking I must say something on every subject and on every occasion.

Release me from craving to try to straighten out everybody's affairs.

Keep my mind free from the recital of endless details; give me wings to get to the point.

I ask for grace enough to listen to the tales of others' pains. Help me to endure them with patience.

But seal my lips on my own aches and pains—they are increasing and my love of rehearsing them is becoming sweater as the years go by.

Teach me the glorious lesson that occasionally it is possible that I may be mistaken.

Keep me reasonably sweet; I do not want to be a saint—some of them are so hard to live with.

Make me thoughtful, but not moody; helpful, but not bossy.

With my vast store of wisdom, it seems a pity not to use it all—but Thou knowest, Lord, that I want a few friends at the end.

—A prayer by an anonymous Mother Superior

INVOLVEMENT: Fitness for older folks

The Goshen (Indiana) College Fitness Center, under the direction of Professor John Ingold, operates a program of physical fitness for men and women of various ages. During the first 2 ½ years of the program, nearly 200 persons took the course. One third were over fifty years and about 8 percent over sixty. The program provides a progressive walk, jog, workout plan. The aim is for persons to keep working out and improving their stamina within their own tested heart range. Some improved, according to the course criteria, more than one hundred percent. All improved some, except one heavy smoker who, while not improving overall, was able to stay with the exercise program and benefit from it.

Three doers. Atlee Beechy, professor of psychology at Goshen College, at age 65 said that by taking the course and continuing the exercises he feels much better physically and psychologically. He jogs from three to four miles twice a week; on the alternate days he carries out the body exercises recommended in the program. These body exercises are listed as trunk rotater, arm circles, bent-knee sit-ups, push-ups, ham string stretcher, arm and leg lifters, leg overs, side leg raises, low-back stretches, and so on. Dr. Beechy feels that he is in good physical condition.

Edna Shantz at sixty-five is part-time professor of home economics at Goshen College. At first she had some apprehension about the fitness course. "I was scared because I thought I was too old to start." Now Edna is a dedicated jogger, jogging three times a week. She comments that the springtime hours in gardening and yard work no longer bring on stiff muscles. "You have to keep body functions working," she says.

Ron Workman owns and operates an insurance agency and took the fitness course in 1977. In 1980 at age sixty-seven he continued to jog, ride a stationary bicycle, do cross-country skiing, bowl, and even helped to set up and play a "beep" baseball game. He recently completed a term as president of the Indiana Rehabilitation Board.

In the summer of 1979 Mr. Workman entered five fun-runs up to ten kilometers each. In one race in which 1,000 runners of all ages were entered, he placed in the middle. These are especially significant achievements for Mr. Workman, since he is blind. Ron runs his races and does his regular jogging with a partner. He has devised a cane, one end of which clips to the belt of his running partner. Ron holds one end of the cane as he follows his partner who is allowed to run freely. Ron also participates with junior high students; as they ride their bicycles, he follows them on the run.

Physical exercise properly supervised can be a boon to older men and women and to the physically disadvantaged if an individual has the discipline to follow such programs.

STARTERS

1
Have you recently walked a mile with an older person? Do it for mutual sheer delight.

2
Help organize an evening of storytelling—humorous and human-interest, song, food that reflects an era, an international theme, or life as it might be twenty-five years from now. Concentrate stories on the tellers' experiences. Include some group calisthenics.

3
You may be aware of an older person attempting to do "too much." Be cautious with advice. Many persons are discouraged from doing what they can and should be doing physically. Be concerned, but show a healthy concern.

4
An older person recovering from a fall, broken bone, or sprain will welcome a get-well card and note, as well as visits. A properly timed visit is an exercise in healing power. You have the capacity to bring cheer.

5
Older people are often ready to try something new, given a little encouragement from family or friends. For instance, some older persons will be ready to learn to swim or to take part in a water exercise class. Why not join the class together?

6
Some older persons denigrate or tell demeaning jokes on themselves. The person may feel, "I'm not important to anyone. Nobody cares." Be an advocate for the older person through friendly confrontation and an understanding ear.

7
Smile. Make a habit of noticing and complimenting persons rather than just asking, "How are you?" Share your happiness and humor.

5 How to Survive Middle Age and Enjoy It, Too

Middle-aged persons have to make many adjustments to life. For one thing, role changes for husbands and wives may not occur at the same time. Women are generally the first to be affected by change. When children leave home the mother's schedule becomes more free—for better or for worse. At this same time husbands are likely to be reaching the peak of their activities in their work, which creates a discrepancy in the responsibilities of husbands and wives.

This may also be the time for boredom on the part of women; many turn to alcohol. Some middle-aged women become problem drinkers making up a significant portion of the 10,000,000 alcoholics in the United States. Marriages which held together largely because of children rather than true compatibility, are often threatened during middle age. However, this could be the time—past the stresses of child-rearing—when marriages become the most meaningful. For good or ill, major readjustment is usually required. Yet few think ahead to this necessity.

A word of caution

Those in the middle-age bracket are busy with some of life's most important functions: making a living, raising a family, carrying major responsibility and leadership for the work of the community, church, and government. Middle-agers face the relentless thrust of competition on the one hand, and on the other begin to realize that the time for the last job promotion is near or past. But even these grave responsibilities can no longer be accepted as valid reasons for avoiding thought and preparation for the next stage in life.

Middle-age malaise

Why don't more middle-aged persons effectively plan for retirement careers? Here are some possibilities:

---

1. We fear the aging process and associate it with weakness and death.
2. We hate to admit that the bloom of life is fading, and that irreversible changes are taking place in us. We fear death and illness, and thus put all thoughts of aging out of our minds.
3. We realize that the time to get ahead—to secure pay raises, promotions, or new jobs—is slipping by rapidly. And we know that if we lose our positions or jobs we will have increasing difficulty getting another one of equal status.
4. We have been in the forefront of economic decisions and raising a family, filling important positions. We don't want to take the time.
5. We are the power structure, the decision-makers, the entrepreneurs, the power brokers, the planners, and we don't want to lose this status.
6. We equate productivity with making money, with adding to the gross national product.
7. We were influenced by the great economic Depression of the thirties and early forties. We were frightened by unemployment—jobs were something special to hold on to.
8. Men do not want to take wives into their confidence and make a full disclosure of economic matters.
9. We may never have taken time to experience leisure and evaluate it honestly.
10. Our parents were rural people and did not have to make extensive plans for retirement. In fact, they may never have completely retired.
11. We have moved from a rural to an industrial economy without recognizing the significant factors of change— mobility, urban living conditions, greater longevity, family size, structure and attitudes, job specifications.
12. We do not realize how close retirement may be and how many years we may have. The fact is some people spend one third of their lives in retirement.

A special word to husbands

"Husbands, love your wives, as Christ loved the church and gave himself up for it" (Eph. 5:25, NEB).

Your wife is likely to live eight years as a widow. At sixty-five the average male may expect to live twelve more years and the female sixteen. Compounding the situation is the fact that husbands are often older than wives. Furthermore, many males do not reach the age of sixty-five. More men than women are taken in the forty to sixty-age bracket by the three great killers—cardiovascular diseases, strokes, and cancer.

If your wife survives you she should know:

1. How much income she could expect. Does either of you have a realistic idea?
2. Have you discussed burial plans, including a plot, or will she need to make these decisions at a time of great trauma?
3. Has your wife had any experience in family finances?
   a. Do you have a joint bank account (or separate ones) so she would have cash available immediately?
   b. Does she know where the key to your safe-deposit box is and how to get to it?
   c. Is she acquainted with the details of the will (which should be jointly executed) or don't you have one? This oversight could be costly and inconvenient.
   d. Does she have a list of your financial obligations— weekly, monthly, yearly—taxes, mortgages, and loans, including installments?
   e. Does she understand your general insurance program, including burial aid?
   f. Is she acquainted with your various types of insurance coverage, car inspection schedules, registrations, and the like?
4. Do you have children or other close relatives or friends to whom she could go for assistance or other surrogates with whom she would feel comfortable?
5. Do you have a family lawyer and is she acquainted with him or her?
6. What should she do with your personal belongings?
7. Can she drive a car (she isn't too old to learn in most cases) and is the car in good mechanical condition?
8. Where will she live? Can she continue to live independently and take care of the premises, including the lawn, trees and shrubs, snow shoveling? Or should she move to a more appropriate facility?

A suggestion to wives

"Wives, respect (understand) your husbands" (Eph. 5:22). When your husband starts a new career (retires) he may become quite disoriented:

1. His job was his daily orientation, probably for many years a daily routine. This structure vanishes overnight. His experience is much like yours when your last child left home. Many of his closest friends were his fellow workers.

2. His work to him was important. His energy and emotional drives were work-centered. Since he no longer has a paying job he may feel a sense of unproductiveness, even worthlessness or guilt.

3. If he has reached the age of sixty-five, many of his closest friends, outside his job, are also gone. Statistically, of our ten closest friends at sixty, three will have died and three moved away by the time we are seventy. Furthermore, your husband likely does not make friends as easily as you do. Unfortunately, our culture trains men to build business relationships and downplays forming other friendships.

4. He is not used to being around the house so much, and you, too, will have adjustments to make. You might find that absence did "make the heart grow fonder," until both of you get used to the new conditions. One wife confessed that she took her husband for better or for worse but not for lunch. Another complained that after her husband's retirement she had twice as much husband and half as much money.

5. You still do the things you regularly did but on a less demanding scale. You continue to cook, experiment with new recipes, sew, knit, tend house plants, garden, and read as you have done for years. But your husband probably does not have many hobbies, nor has he learned how to experience leisure creatively.

Realism and advocacy

Paul E. Johnson in *The Middle Years* (Fortress Press, 1971) calls for a sense of frank realism in middle age, admitting to ourselves that we can't go back to childhood. It doesn't help to daydream trying to undo what we have done, or do what we might have done to erase our mistakes, Johnson observes. We should expend our energy in finding a better way to the future and not shrink from accepting the fact that we are growing older. This is God's plan for our lives. There is a peculiar beauty in every age, open to new life and new experience. Our best at any age can be done only as we allow our potential to be fulfilled in concert with others.

When the middle-aged act as advocates for the elderly they are only a step away from helping themselves. They will soon need the same understanding and concern.

In those societies where there is some degree of equality—with a rural community, for example, or among certain primitive nations—the middle-aged man is aware, in spite of himself, that his state tomorrow will be the same as that which he allots to the old today. That is the meaning of Grimm's tale, versions of which are to be found in every countryside. A peasant makes his old father eat out of a small wooden trough, apart from the rest of the family; one day he finds his son fitting little boards together. "It's for you when you are old," says the child. Straightaway the grandfather is given back his place at the family table.
—Simone De Beauvoir in *The Coming of Age* (Warner Books)

Survival by learning, learning, learning

Education is ongoing in life, not something which we finish once and for all. Persons no longer prepare for a career but for careers. Many children now in elementary school will work at jobs which now do not even exist, completely new careers. Technology makes many jobs obsolescent. The telephone operator placing each individual call is long since gone. Young people do not know what elevator operators look like. The bookkeeper has given way to the computer.

What kind of an education will it take to respond to the needs of a person who quits an earning career at age fifty-five, or one who works twenty-eight hours a week with three months' vacation plus the holidays—more days off the job than on? What kind of an education will be most useful to the person who typically will be underemployed for a period of time, then employed for a shortened period of meaningful and self-satisfying work, and then retired at the height of social, intellectual, and psychological productivity?

In our new mass-educated society, underemployment will be endemic. As educators review their tasks, it will become apparent that most workers will need three kinds of learning: (1) a tangible skill for what it is hoped will be the short-term job of relatively menial character, (2) the broad educational underpinnings for a variety of eventually challenging work, and (3) the capacity to fulfill oneself apart from the job. I hope those who administer and teach in schools, colleges, and universities will bear this in mind as they work out the relative emphasis to place on welding, economics, and the violin.
—Francis I. Fisher, Director Career Services and Off Campus Learning, Harvard University

This means that education, formal and informal, must not push us into straightiackets. In college it might mean interdisciplinary majors covering three fields. Reason, judgment, common sense, and general knowledge, as well as specific knowledge, versatility, adaptability, and ethical and spiritual priorities, will have to be emphasized. Such an education must equip us to move with ease from one situation to another, laterally or vertically. It must help individuals to know what to do when they are alone, as well as how to act in groups in the great period of free time ahead. Free time must be turned into constructive leisure-time pursuits of value to the individual and society.

Some specific learnings to acquire

1. Get perspective—where do I aim to be in twenty, thirty, or forty years?

2. Make your lifestyle one of flexibility and openness to change. Nothing is more sure than change. Flexibility and lack of ethical principles are not synonymous. Aged persons of today have had to adapt to an incredible number of changes. Stubborn, complaining, unhappy persons at twenty-five, thirty-five, or forty-five are likely to be the same at sixty-five. The gift of long life may be a bitter fruit for those who will not accommodate themselves to change.

Prayer: "Lord, give me long life only if it is filled with purpose and meaning."

3. How shall we find the road to fulfillment in old age?

1. Be realistic and face the facts of life.
2. Develop your potential for more effective relationships with others; help others.
3. Examine your dormant gifts, talents, resources, long-time interests; seek the opinion of your peers in assessing your gifts.
4. Increase your creative productivity. Start something new even if you are not sure of being successful. Low aim is more tragic than missing the mark.
5. Exercise social concern—get involved.
6. Make an effort to understand and participate with youth; interact with all ages. This can be done through family, church, and community structures.
7. Focus your life outward. Reach out!
8. Husband and wife should plan together. Seek the counsel of others.
9. Begin hobbies. Waiting until sixty-five may be a bit late. Start searching today.
10. Learn how to use leisure; start practicing. Mix leisure and work, and make it a part of your lifestyle.
11. Spiritual resources must be cultivated throughout life to be most useful in later years.
12. Start to think in terms of what can be done by oneself. Many people have learned what to do when they are with others without knowing what to do when they are alone.
13. Make it a way of life to give new suggestions a fair hearing. Do not use a negative approach. Try to see what's right rather than what's wrong.
14. We should take our daily work and witness seriously without taking ourselves too seriously. We should be able to laugh at ourselves, to recognize how stupid and foolish some of our actions may have been. At times we should verbally and honestly confess, "I was wrong."
15. No ready-made plans or answers fit all retirement cases. There is no such thing as a pair of shoes for a typical sixty-five-year-old person. In fact, there aren't any typical persons. We have to make our own plans. We cannot use, in most cases, the plans our parents followed, or even those of our peers.
16. We should learn as much as possible about ourselves and the aging process including the biological, social, psychological, and spiritual areas.

17. We should learn how to forgive and to be forgiven. Continued resentment in our hearts is a crushing load we can't afford to carry.

Building friendships

Friendships are important for everyone, but particularly for older persons, because as each year passes so do friends. When we reach retirement years, our sphere of influence becomes more compressed and the kind acts of friends become more and more important.

INVOLVEMENT: Extending the family

Doris and Ivan Gascho of Kitchener, Ontario, in 1978 began a new living arrangement which involved her parents, a cousin, and other unrelated persons. They weighed family, economic, and religious-faith-in-practice factors before moving ahead with changes suited to the responsibility, planning, and adjustments of middle age. They describe how they came to set up a living arrangement to cope with these new circumstances:

Time for a move. Doris's parents had immediate needs such as home upkeep and related responsibilities which were becoming more difficult to handle. With some support services they would still be able to live independently and with more enjoyment. "We broached the subject on occasion," Doris said.

The Gaschos themselves found the cost of heating and maintaining their 170-year-old home mounting. With only one child left at home they did not need as much space anymore. Ivan's business no longer operated from that location. Doris's work and the majority of the family's outside activities occurred in the city six miles distant.

Doris and Ivan had a vague sense of wanting to try an intentional neighbor style of living, which would include sharing appliances, car, and so on.

Factors considered. Conditions for a change included concerns to live near, but not with Doris's parents. Doris and Ivan wanted space for entertaining. They wanted to be within walking distance of bus and shopping, drugstore and post office.

The Gaschos still needed bedrooms for the children until they established their own homes. They looked for parking space for guests and an easy driveway. The cost of housing had to be within their means, provide adequate storage space, and offer garden space. Finally, the place should require little repair or decorating.

The search. Doris and Ivan first looked for a semi-detached home (double home). Nothing suitable was available. They looked at a triplex. It had three apartments over each other with one partially below ground; two apartments had two bedrooms. It met most of their criteria and bordered a park.

They continued their search, checking out other buildings. They talked about the triplex with Doris's parents who were then in Florida. "Whatever you choose is okay," they said. Six months after they began the search the Gaschos bought the triplex. Doris and Ivan moved into two of the apartments. A week after their move the triplex next door—identical in design and construction—came up for sale. They decided to buy it. Doris's parents moved into the ground-level apartment of the second building.

Tenants. Other tenants in the two buildings in early 1980 included two single fellows, a widow in her seventies, and a younger widow who is Doris's cousin. The group decided to start with a few agreements and let "intentional neighborhood" evolve. Early common events included a meal every two weeks, which was later changed to coffee every three weeks. "In this two-hour time period we tell what we've been doing, mention any prayer concerns, have prayer, and continue sharing," Doris said.

Parents' response. They can call the landlord. They miss the trees, the view, the lawn, but are glad not to have to take care of all that. They couldn't find things in the new grocery store at first. They have the same activities as before. It is important to them to have harmony in the building—similar lifestyles. People coming and going feel like extended family.

"Dad is glad for the workshop, both for space and tools," said Doris. "We often say to the folks, 'Have you got supper on? Come over, we have a big pot of soup.' Sometimes we invite the fellows downstairs in for a meal."

Snags. Interest rates climbed higher than anticipated. Rental increases were pegged at a maximum 6 percent increase. Doris was uneasy about "landlording"; Ivan wasn't. He'd talked to other landlords and knew what to expect. He has an easygoing way about tenants' needs and takes time to talk with them. Finding the right tenants was easier than they expected. Word of mouth, as well as newspaper want ads, got persons in touch with each other.

Sharing. For guests, extra pots and pans and chairs are passed around. Gift plants go to a common flower bed. A tiny garden provides flowers, fresh lettuce, and zucchini. Leftovers are shared as are TV specials, projects needing an extra pair of hands, advice, shopping buggy. Anxieties and joys fall on receptive ears.

With the time and thought they have given to their basic questions and interests, Doris and Ivan are better equipped to deal with other adjustments. They are also better prepared for the joys, questions, and opportunities of daily life. They are enjoying their family, their extended household, church, work, and themselves. Doris sometimes walks her daughter the 1 ½ miles to high school. "Good chatting time," Doris said, "and a good time for walking the dog."

STARTERS
"Be nice to yourselves once in a while, but not too nice," is good advice as you move through middle age. At the same time, encourage and support older persons in the experiences that provide rewarding interaction, activity, and reflection for them.

A word to older persons
You are a VIP, a very important person. God made you that way. You have done many good things for your neighbors, your friends, your family. You have made economic and social sacrifices. Many a time you kept bedside vigil during the sickness

of a child. During the Depression your budget was so tight you bought only the bare necessities. You, perhaps, became more accustomed to give than to receive. Here are some suggestions to encourage you to receive as well as give:

1

Your children are adults and probably started their career on a higher economic plane than you ever reached. Don't think that you must save for them; except in special cases, they won't need it. Give more to the church institutions and to other worthwhile and trustworthy charities.

2

It may be the time to take a "honeymoon" trip, the one you couldn't afford to take when you got married, or do other significant traveling, or buy yourself a new dress or a new suit. You should feel a sense of well-being and live in reasonable comfort, use labor-saving devices, wear neat and comfortable clothing without feelings of guilt.

3

Make real friends of your children and grandchildren by doing the kinds of things with them that don't require money. Grandchildren say "ideal" grandparents are loving, gentle, helpful, friends, understanding, industrious, smart, talkative, funny.

4.

"Eat out" once in a while to experience a new environment and also to recognize how good your own cooking really is. But eating out should be more than a conversation piece—a status symbol—and more than an exercise in finding how many new places may be within certain geographic boundaries.

5

Avoid being too nice or too easy with yourself. Discipline your habits, eating, physical output, and material urges. On the other hand, avoid being too hard on yourself as though you were unworthy of the fullness with which you were created. Get proper exercise; read demanding books, newspapers, and magazines; use the dictionary, the encyclopedia, Bible concordance, and a Bible dictionary regularly. Travel to learn, to appreciate God's vast creation and the beauty of nature; travel with a purpose. Your greatest fulfillment socially and spiritually should come from helping others, as well as drawing on the meanings of your own devotional life.

6

For women who have never driven a car, now is the time to learn. Even women in their seventies are learning to drive. Forty-two percent of those sixty-five and above in Indiana do not drive a car. Most of these women are women who depended on their husbands for transportation.

7

Above all, do not fall for the old stereotype of society that you are a "has-been," that you have to loaf mentally and physically to fulfill your role, that you have to leave a comfortable nest egg to your next of kin to prove your worth. Remember, the attitude you model will likely convey itself to your children and help create a new appreciation for the older VIP you are.

Don't Expect a Flowery Bed of Ease

It is nowhere promised or implied that life will be a bowl of cherries, or bed of roses free from thorns. Isaac Watts asked in a hymn written in 1721, "Must I be carried to the skies on flowery beds of ease, while others fought to win the prize or sailed through bloody seas?" The answer was "No" then, as it is now. To go through life without strain and stress would keep us weak and immature.

The apostle Paul reported "being caught up into the third heaven" and receiving some wonderful revelations. He said, "And to keep me from being too elated [puffed up by pride] by the abundance of revelations, a thorn [a sharp pain in the side] was given me in the flesh. Three times I besought the Lord about this, that it should leave me; but he said to me, 'My grace is sufficient for you, for my power is made perfect in weakness' " (2 Corinthians 12:7,8). Paul recognized that stress, pain, and tension will come but there is an answer: "We are afflicted in every way, but not crushed; perplexed, but not driven to despair; persecuted, but not forsaken; struck down, but not destroyed" (2 Corinthians 4:8,9).

Paul also said: "So we do not lose heart. Though our outer nature is wasting away, our inner nature is being renewed every day" (2 Corinthians 4:16). "I know how to be abased, and I know how to abound; in any and all circumstances I have learned the secret of facing plenty and hunger, abundance and want" (Philippians 4:12).

Strain is common to all, but some are more vulnerable

Stress and strain strike everyone regardless of age. Children go through many stress periods, especially with our fragile family structures. However, older persons are exceptionally vulnerable. The ultimate example of inability to cope with stress is suicide. One third of all suicides in the United States are by persons over age 65. The suicide rate is increasing most rapidly with older men. Many older women also attempt suicide, but fewer attempts are successful. While the percentage of elderly suicides increases, the numbers are small.

Active society rejects the man who has retired. Intellectually and sociologically, he becomes less and less involved and interested in the problems of the world; he feels that he will never live to see any of them solved. Most devastatingly of all, he is lonely. His wife may have died or grown apart in interest and intellect over the years; his children are either scattered or married with children of their own in a family unit in which he feels a burden—an extra wheel. In short, there is a general feeling that one of the great horrors of growing old is that one ceases to be of any use.
—Jack Gurley in *Life After 65*

Function for stress

Stress and strain are important.

The word *stress* frightens many people, particularly middle-aged and older adults. Yet stress is an important factor in keeping the mind and body functioning normally. Too many people believe that good health depends on how easy things are, that an individual's health and happiness directly relate to how little effort is required to live.

Everyone, particularly older people, should realize the difference between abnormal or injurious stress and the moderate everyday stress which is so vital to maintaining normal body function.
—In *More Life for Your Years* (June 19, 1971), copyright 1971, American Medical Association

---

The American Medical Association Committee on Aging feels that the key to positive health lies in indulging in the stress of living, rather than avoiding it. Biologically speaking, the wounds of combat are by far preferable to the decay that comes from remaining idle.

Learn to master stress

Dr. Hans Selye, probably the world's greatest authority on stress, said: "Complete freedom from stress is death. Don't try to avoid stress—it's the very salt and spice of life. But learn to master and to use it." He pointed out that we shouldn't try to avoid stress but pick the right kind: "There are two kinds— distress (from *dis* meaning bad) and eustress (*eu* meaning good as in euphoria or eulogy). Thus stress can be either good or bad, helpful or hurtful.

Be selective in your worries

An older person, when asked what he might do differently in a reappraisal of his life, said, "I would be more selective in my worries." We become too involved in too many concerns and then become frustrated. Tension directed to rightful concern can be beneficial.

Is tension bad for you? Judging from the number of people in compulsive pursuit of recreation and relaxation these days, you might conclude that the only alternative is ulcers and a program of psychiatric therapy. The truth is that *mental stress* is not dangerous to your health unless you make a *career of it.* Indeed, tension has some desirable attributes and it might be a good thing if more people were willing to take advantage of them. For example, tension prepares you for action. It produces the adrenalin that helps mobilize mind and body for the extra effort needed to solve problems that really matter. Have you ever heard of a serious problem being solved by relaxation?

—In *More Life for Your Years* (October, 1971), copyright 1971, American Medical Association

---

Recognizing stress

Any symptom that is unusual for you can indicate stress. Worrying about symptoms can itself cause stress.

Here is a listing of some common symptoms of stress:
1. **Tense muscles, sore neck, shoulders, and back. These conditions may lead to headache or backache.**
2. **Insomnia—difficulty in falling asleep or staying asleep.**
3. **Fatigue—if not brought on by extreme physical exertion.**
4. **Boredom, depression, listlessness, dullness, and lack of interest—a person constantly in these states is under stress which saps energy.**
5. **Drinking to escape problems.**
6. **Eating too much or too little.**
7. **Diarrhea, cramps, gas, chest pains.**
8. **Palpitations—heart skip. As stress increases the heartbeat, a cycle of fear or stress alarm results.**
9. **Phobia—unfounded fear.**
10. **Tics, restlessness, itching.**

> —From *Coping with Stress,* a bulletin issued by Oaklawn
> Mental Health Center, Elkhart, Indiana

Stress through longer marriages

Family situations have changed greatly during the past century. Husband and wife can expect forty-five years of married life together—three times longer than a century ago. The last child typically leaves home after the parents have been married less than thirty years, and many parents face twenty or more years of married life living alone. During this "empty nest" period many changes in family relationships take place. The last child leaving home can be traumatic for the mother somewhat like the loss of a job or retirement for the father. This experience of less responsibility with children gone, along with the middle-age change of life, comes when the husband is reaching his highest level of financial and social responsibility and prestige. This becomes a dangerous period in family relationships. Many divorces take place during this time, and the rate is accelerating. This often happens in families where there had been no public indication that anything was wrong. This middle-age period has become one of the most troubled and unstable for many American families and a rich and rewarding one for others.

A new approach must be developed to help couples adjust

to this longer period together with its many facets of change. Many middle-aged and older couples need counseling to become informed and thus understand what is happening and what will likely continue to take place. Biologically, couples who live longer face changes in later life which couples who died at younger ages never experienced. These may include decreases in hearing, sight, sexual drive, and positions of power and prestige. Adjustments for longer life together have to be made even though many persons never have learned the art of compromise and care. Couples must learn patience, more forbearance, acceptance of aging in themselves and in their partners, flexibility, and the need to accept counsel and aid from the outside. There may be periods of hospitalization, physical impairment, and mental lapses which call for a deep quality of love and understanding— situations which most younger persons have seldom if ever experienced.

Marriage counseling

We commonly think of marriage counseling in terms of premarital sessions or as dealing with families and children. We will need to extend our concept of marriage counseling to include helping older persons cope with this long and comparatively new period of togetherness. Society, and particularly the church, needs to understand what is happening in older families and consider how the church actually functions as the body of Christ in these transitional situations.

Remarriage counseling

Another need for counseling is in the area of remarriage for formerly married persons. In the U.S. at this time, there are approximately 8,000,000 widows and 2,000,000 widowers, most of whom are older persons. Twice as many older men as older women remarry. Between 1960 and 1973, the number of older men and older women who remarried doubled.

This trend for increased remarriages of older persons will probably accelerate. Persons over sixty-five today are in better health and better financial condition, are better educated formally and informally, and have traveled more widely than ever before. With more ways to get acquainted and more social opportunities available, persons who haven't completely forgotten about romance may have their banked fires rekindled.

Remarriage in the later years is a viable option under many circumstances. However, counseling should be made available and publicized so that those contemplating remarriage may realize such service is for them.

These persons are apt to be more coy and reserved about romance than younger persons are currently. Also they may not realize that infatuation tends to play tricks, even to those who consider themselves veterans in the art.

Remarriage in the later years is one of the least researched alternatives for older persons. Recent studies by the American Medical Association indicated that such marriages are viable and generally successful (1) if the first marriages were good ones, (2) if the couple knew each other for a period of years, (3) if they married for companionship and love, and (4) if they have the approval of their children. The studies also showed that for older persons remarrying, income is not of most importance; good health is very important; and marriage adds years through better diet, mutual care, and by avoiding accidents because there are two pairs of eyes and ears.

A life-events stress scale

Dr. Thomas A. Holmes, a psychiatrist, and his colleagues at the University of Washington School of Medicine in Seattle developed a "life-events scale" (below) designed to measure the psychological stress that can be caused by various changes in life circumstances. It is said that the scale provides a "reasonably good correlation" between life changes and onset of depression and medical problems.

Studies by Dr. Holmes indicate that an accumulation of 200 or more "life-change units" in a single year may be more disruption than an individual can withstand—and make him vulnerable to illness.

Event	Scale of Impact
Death of spouse	100
Divorce	73
Marital separation	65
Jail term	63

Death of close family member	63
Personal injury or illness	53
Marriage	50
Fired at work	47
Marital reconciliation	45
Retirement	45
Change in health of family member	44
Pregnancy	40
Sex difficulties	39
Gain of new family member	39
Business readjustment	39
Change to different line of work	36
Change in number of arguments with spouse	35
Mortgage over $10,000	31
Foreclosure of mortgage or loan	30
Change in responsibilities at work	29
Son or daughter leaving home	29
Trouble with in-laws	29
Outstanding personal achievement	28
Wife begins or stops work	26
Begin or end school	25
Revision of personal habits	24
Trouble with boss	23
Change in residence	20
Change in schools	20
Change in recreation	19
Change in church activities	19
Change in social activities	18
Mortgage or loan less than $10,000	17
Change in sleeping habits	16
Change in number of family get-togethers	15
Change in eating habits	15
Vacation	13
Christmas	12
Minor violation of the law	11

INVOLVEMENT: A healthy destiny in human sexuality

To many Americans sex has become an obsession—an aberration. In one TV program a half-dozen middle-aged men and women were interviewed regarding their future. In appraising their future, without exception, each of the interviewees felt that the physical bloom of life was fading, that they would continue to become less attractive physically, and that their sex life would become less intense. Nothing was said about moral, social, or spiritual expectations or lifestyles which would help them become whole persons.

Reuel Howe (*How to Stay Younger While Growing Older,* pp. 11-13), recorded conversations at a workshop on aging which he attended. Howe said he was twenty years older than any other attendee and his presence was resented. One man asked him what he was doing there, and Howe said he was there because he wanted to grow. The man, seemingly both fearful and angry, finally asked Howe, "Do you have any fun anymore?" Howe asked the inquirer to be more explicit and he said, "Do you have sex anymore?" Howe told him, "Of course I enjoy the comforts and pleasures of sex." At the conclusion of the conference Howe was thanked for proving "that as old as you are there can be some satisfactions in life" (probably meaning sex).

The late Stephen Jewett, MD, of New York Medical College interviewed seventy-nine persons aged eighty-seven to 103 years. He found that there were many common factors in their longevity. Nearly all had been married and 60 percent still lived as married couples. They remained sexually active and disproved the myth that sex was harmful in later years. Yet myths linger. Physician Willard S. Krabill of Goshen, Indiana, in the section which follows, gives some of the foundation stones on which he bases his efforts to help people achieve a positive attitude toward human sexuality.

HUMAN SEXUALITY
By Willard S. Krabill, MD

My observations through twenty years of medical practice—a practice concentrated first in family practice, then obstetrics and gynecology, and now college health—indicate that the decisions and practices and attitudes we choose now determine what our tomorrow will be in human sexuality. Our right decisions today about the place of sex in our life and our uses of sex can bless our future days tremendously. And our wrong decisions today about our uses and purposes in sex can blight our tomorrow in myriads of ways.

Human sexuality refers to all those facets of the human personality and the human body which collectively identify us as male or female—not just genital sex or sexual intercourse. We

are all (all the time) sexual beings and are therefore all creating
our destiny in human sexuality. Let me suggest some of the foundation stones needed upon which to build a healthy human
sexuality.

Theology of the body. I believe the first foundation stone is a
proper theology of the body. Over the centuries a false
dichotomy has crept into the church's message which suggested
that the body is evil, the spirit is good. Somehow we've grown up
thinking it's wrong to enjoy and feel good about our bodies—
really about ourselves, for in our bodies we are ourselves. We say
that we believe in the wholeness of persons; that we're body,
mind, and spirit; and that preaching, teaching, and healing are all
valid ministries. We talk a lot about holistic health concepts, and
yet we go right on overeating, overworking, overpreaching, over-
sitting around, over-driving our cars, over-"spectatoring," and so
on. However, nowhere is our failure to have a proper attitude
toward our bodies more deleterious than in our negative attitude
toward our sexuality.

James Nelson, in his book *Embodiment,* skillfully pointed
out the multiple ways in which we betray negative attitudes
toward our bodies. We talk about carnal bodies and spiritual
minds. We misunderstand Galatians 5 and confuse flesh with our
physical body. Furthermore, if my body is evil and not really me,
then I can't be held as responsible for the wrong things that my
body does. "I just couldn't help it, you know. I had this
'overwhelming drive' or this 'raging passion.' " When one's body
ceases to be fully personal, Nelson says, relationships to other
body/selves are diminished. If my body isn't good and isn't fully
me, then neither is your body something I need to hold sacred.
So I can more easily use your body, or abuse mine.

Our false theology of the body also keeps us from speaking
openly and honestly about our bodies, including our sexual
bodies. It is always amazing to me how many married couples
have slept together for years and have raised a family, yet have
not even once been able to talk with each other about their
bodies—about their sexual feelings and preferences. Not once!

Our false theology of the body is one of the things which
makes us uptight and unable to touch each other. An affec-

tionate touch or a hug is misread as an invitation to bed, or as a lustful gesture. And in this attitude we hurt our single persons more than we ever realize. We pay a high price for a false theology of the body.

A theology of sexuality. The second foundation stone follows closely and naturally—that is, a proper sexual theology. Do we really believe and understand that sex is good—that our sexuality is a gift from God? We could have, you know, reproduced in some other way. God could easily have arranged that. But no, he created us the way we are.

The church has allowed some harmful misconceptions and false attitudes to creep into its sexual message over the centuries. We don't have a good track record in dealing with those who are hurting in this area of their lives. But a brief glance around the sex saturated, sexually permissive, negativistic sexual wilderness of our day and our culture reveals quickly that the prophets of our hedonistic culture have a poorer track record yet. Those who know the Creator best should reflect best the true nature of human sexuality. Let the message become loud and clear that our sexuality is a source of true joy, of healing, of love, of caring, of unselfishness. Let's renew our search of the Scriptures, finding there positive principles of human sexuality.

Male and female. A third foundation stone is a proper understanding of the equality of males and females. The "papa is all" mentality doesn't fit with a proper sexual theology and should be abandoned. We've yet to understand fully how biologically, developmentally, and physiologically alike male and female are. Where we're not alike we are either equal or complementary. There should be no room for the double standard in Christian circles. However, just as black leaders used to tell us that America is never so racially segregated as it is on Sunday morning, might it not also be said that America is never so sexist-oriented as it is on Sunday morning? God created us sexual, male and female, each unable to exist without the other.

A teacher asked the children in his class to write anything they pleased about people. A little pigtailed girl wrote: "People are composed of two kinds, boys and girls. Boys are no good at all until they grow up and get married. Boys are an awful bother. They want everything but soap. A woman is a grown-up girl with children. My dad is such a nice man that I am sure he must have been a little girl when he was a boy."

Integrating our sexuality. The fourth foundation piece upon which we can build a healthy sexuality and a happy sexual destiny is the understanding that our sexuality is an integral part of who we are. It is part and parcel of the totality of life. Our sexuality is that pervasive essence of our personality that defines us first as human, and second as male or female. Because we relate to others as sexual persons doesn't mean that we have genital sex in mind, but that we simply all the time are sexual beings. Sexuality is an aspect of our lives which cannot be compartmentalized or treated separately.

The marital sexual relationship shows how sexuality is related to the rest of us. A successful sexual experience begins when the couple gets up in the morning. The attitudes, the caring, the tenderness, the messages communicated all day long, whether they are ostensibly about finances, about the children's lessons, about the in-laws, about the cold soup and the soggy pie crust— these are all the prelude to yet another message—a message of "love."

Marriage counselors estimate that when couples come with sexual problems, 80 percent of the time the problem is not really sexual. It may be financial, the matter of an allowance, in-laws, tension and dissension over disciplining the children, personal hygiene, or a combination of these and other problems. Because of such tensions in the marriage, the sexual relationship suffers, and then receives the blame.

Affirming the sexuality of all. The fifth foundation stone is the affirmation of the sexuality of *all* people. Let me illustrate our problem here by noting the way we deny the sexuality of our own parents. The mechanism of this denial probably goes something like this: "Sex is dirty; my parents are nice people; therefore my parents are not sexual."

Let's remember that we cannot and should not deny the sexuality of anyone—male or female, young or old, parents or children, the ill and the handicapped, the brilliant and the dull, *and* the married and the single.

According to Donald Goergen in *The Sexual Celibate,* "A celibate person is not asexual. He or she has a full sexual life which needs to be understood in order to have a richer understanding of Christian sexuality itself as well as in order to assist people in living a celibate life. . . . The sexual life of a celibate person is going to manifest itself primarily in the affective bonds of permanent and steadfast human friendships which are exemplifications of God's way of loving. Through a rediscovery of friendship within the Christian tradition and through an integration of community, friendship, ministry, and prayer, the present discussion of celibacy can lead to a revival of a truly Christian value, the value of friendship, which is a service for the entire Christian community."

Included in the term "everyone" are our older people. We not only desexualize our older members, we depersonalize them as well. Have you ever noticed how an aide, an orderly, a nurse, or a physician will go up to some older person in a hospital or nursing home and patronizingly say, "Now, Susie, don't be so messy"? And did you ever notice how we adopt the attitude that older people have no sexual feelings, no sexual needs, no need for affection? We've even forced elderly married couples to live apart in some institutional settings.

What leadership is the church giving in recognizing and affirming the sexuality of our older members? Or are we remaining dumb in the face of a culture, families, and institutions which depersonalize and desexualize our aging population? Why can't affection-starved residents in retirement homes have a lounge where they can date, or why can't we tolerate those nursing home residents touching, holding hands, or occasionally hugging without being labeled?

Learning about sex. The sixth foundation piece for creating our sexual destiny is that of sound sex education. Our understandings about human sexuality and our sexual attitudes are learned, and as such they need to be communicated by the best teachers available. Sound sex education is imperative to our creating a happy sexual destiny. The first element found in sound sex education is loving, affectionate, communicating parents who are able to talk about their sexuality with ease and candor and whose own sexual lifestyle is Christian.

Ideally, the second element is a caring, loving congregation. As Helen Kruger says, "If the church remains silent on the subject of sexuality, its very silence will say that sex is beneath the dignity of Christian teaching.... Children especially need values before they are immersed in the hedonistic world of *Playboy* and television, and before they are emotionally (passionately) involved themselves."

Third, sex education may need to be supplemented in the schools for many in our society. I think it is needed and I think we shouldn't oppose it. I hope, however, that Christian parents through the home and the church will have already given their children a good sex education, including sexual values, before the children confront the education model in the public schools.

In addition to the foregoing elements of social sex education, other important concepts must be communicated. One is that our sexuality is a wonderful gift from God. It is a *good* thing. It is given for our pleasure. We can misuse it, so it requires care, responsibility, and maturity. In growing up sexually, we need first of all to establish our identity before tackling intimacy. We see on all sides the tragic results in young lives of having found intimacy before finding identity. And you never really "grow up," no matter how old you are, until you are willing to accept responsibility for someone else's happiness.

Another important message is that sexuality is far more than anatomy, physiology, and the sexual response system. Sex is most of all a matter of communication, relationship, and commitment.

Further, whatever else can be said about it, sex is not "casual." The sexual behavior of those who consider it as casual as sharing a Coke, or holding hands, are exhibiting a denial of their basic humanity. Their behavior is crude and animalistic, and to me it is not *human* sexuality—neither in its character nor in its potential.

Celebrate sex. The last foundation stone is that sex is to be celebrated. Sex is for rejoicing; sex is joy; sex is happiness; sex is fulfillment for everyone at all ages. How beautiful a dimension it was for God to create sexuality. The Bible even likens the marital relationship to the relationship of Christ and his church.

Someone has said that those who are mentally and emotionally healthy are those who have learned to say three things: They have learned when to say *yes*; when to say *no*; and when to say *whoopee*! Let each of us affirm that our sexuality is one of the whoopees of our lives.

STARTERS

Here are some helpful ways of living with stress:

1

Look for causes. Who or what is at the bottom of the stress? Dealing directly with the person or issue may be the best approach.

2

Examine your relationships. What can you do to put more warmth, more communication, and more mutual support into them?

3

Evaluate. Not every argument is worth trying to win. Defend values that are important, but learn to ignore lesser issues.

4

Be positive. If you fail, don't concentrate on failure. Deliberately recall past successes. It helps self-esteem.

5

Seek advice. Confiding in a friend can uncoil the tightly wound spring of tension. Seek professional assistance when needed. You're worth it.

6

Do something for others. Reaching out can take the focus off self and reduce the stress caused by brooding.

7

Do one thing at a time. The seconds pass in single file. Yet how quickly they become minutes and hours. You'll get more done with less hassle when you concentrate on each job as it comes.

8

Learn to pace yourself. You can't operate in high gear all the time. Take a break. Go for a walk. Look out the window. Do something else.

9

Exercise. Physical exercise can refresh you after heavy mental work. Reading a book can relax you after demanding physical action.

10

Create a quiet place. Take time to meditate, to pray.

—From *Christopher News Notes*

7 Hats Off to Retirement Careers

The work ethic is firmly embedded within us. In meeting a person for the first time, particularly a man, we are apt to ask:
1. What is your name?
2. Where do you live?
3. Who are your parents? We spar for some identity, hoping to pick up some common stakes such as, "I used to live there and I knew so and so." Or possibly the name might bring out the fact that you could be related and who of us overlooks an opportunity to expand on this theme?
4. What do you do? This is the question we've really been leading up to. A man is likely to expand on the status of his job—probably making it more glamorous than is justified. He enjoys pointing out that he is gainfully employed, paying taxes, making his own way, and getting along fine without being dependent on others. If the woman is a homemaker, she may say, "I am just a housewife. However, I do a good deal of community service and voluntary work in both church and community."

The worth ethic
We should consider retirement a new career in which we think about the *worth* ethic as opposed to the work ethic. In retirement careers we are offered opportunities for some of the most creative and meaningful life experiences, the chance to find self-fulfillment, to serve, to build self-esteem, to explore new lifestyles, and to attain greater spiritual growth. Older persons can do many worthwhile things for which those who are fully

employed do not have time—things which really count.

In answer to the question about what they do, few will say, "I don't do anything, and I don't give a hoot about what anyone thinks." Generally, older persons are very conscious about their replies and embarrassed to say that they don't do anything. Even though they no longer add to the Gross National Product, they don't want to be forced to say that they are nonproductive. Society must be reeducated to accept the idea that a creative use of free time is a worthy use of leisure. We must also learn that many activities are productive even though capital goods are not created.

Thomas Jefferson, who at the age of sixty-eight resumed a serious study of mathematics, stated, "There is a fullness of time when men should go and not occupy too long the ground to which others have a right to advance." Retirement is not the cessation of activity, but rather the opportunity for persons to determine individually how time is to be used. It is the time in the curriculum of life when we move to electives from required courses. Retirement careers mark the beginning of something new, not the end. They are an exclamation mark, not a period.

The meanings of work: A closer look*

Because of our common experience, work is a familiar concept to North Americans. In everyday terminology, work, labor, and toil mean much the same thing. Labor in a sense denoted strenuous physical exertion in the past. We have gotten far past the concept, however, that work is something we do with our hands.

We work—
1. **To provide for life's necessities.**
2. **To maintain a standard of living.**
3. **To satisfy psychological needs.**
4. **To establish an identification and a status. A man's sense of worth is frequently tied directly to the job he holds. A psychiatrist at Rockland State Mental Hospital, Orangeburg, New York, said, "Most people in our culture work—if they are fortunate—not just to make**

---

*Many of the suggestions on work and leisure came from Harold Lehman's excellent book, *In Praise of Leisure,* Herald Press, 1974.

money but because they derive satisfaction from what
they are doing."
5. **Because it promises future benefits.** We work partly because of deferred benefits; a future time orientation.
6. **Because it supplies moral satisfactions.** Rewards for
faithful labor are promised both in this world and the
next. Some persons feel that work may be a kind of
divinely ordained system of measuring and rewarding
human worth.

Women working outside the home

There has been an increasing trend for women to work outside the home for wages. Actually, this is not new. Among rural
people, many women throughout history worked at farm duties.
Their physical labors in the home with primitive equipment, their
large families, poor medical attention particularly at childbirth—
such conditions caused many premature female deaths.
However, these labors were not considered financially remunerative.

Women have never received just financial compensation for
their contributions to family life.

With the advent of labor-saving devices in the home,
smaller families, better transportation, better education, the
breaking down of prejudices, the availability of jobs, political
rights, the rising standard of living with certain lifestyles made
possible by two family incomes, the trend toward female
remunerative employment continues.

The following schedule showing the percentage of
women working outside the home is significant:
1920: 23 percent
1950: 34 percent
1960: 37 percent
1970: 43 percent
1980: over 50 percent

From 1960 to 1980 the increase has been especially significant. Women now make up 41.9 percent of the total work force
in the United States. Forty-seven percent of married women
work outside the home. During the seventies the number of

working wives increased to the point where 8.5 million families were solely supported by women.

The Protestant work ethic

Max Weber in the early 1900s developed his classic theory linking Protestantism and capitalism. He observed that in Protestant countries capitalism made its swiftest headway, with Calvinists and Puritans providing a large proportion of the new entrepreneurs. To the Calvinist business was a serious and exacting enterprise to be pursued with a sense of religious responsibility. Work was not only an economic means but a spiritual end. To be on earth was to be responsible to work.

Max Weber commented on the combination of religious ways of life and the intensive development of business acumen which characterized the Quakers and Mennonites—both of whom were known for their otherworldliness and wealth. Val Royer, writing on Church of the Brethren economic ethic, observes that the Brethren and Mennonites in America appear to pursue with even greater intensity and devotion the economic activities of life than did the Calvinists, probably as a result of their social and political isolation.

In Puritan society, work was legitimized as a means of glorifying God and was held up as a defense against idleness and waste of time. Diligence, thrift, and sobriety were cardinal virtues. The story is told of a Puritan woman who was waiting in a darkened room for the funeral services for her deceased husband to begin. Not wishing to waste a minute in idleness she whispered to her daughter, "Pass thee my knitting. I might knit a few bouts while the folks are gathering."

Longevity alters family circumstances

In the typical family in 1900 (with large families and earlier deaths), one of the parents died before the last child left home. There were few "empty nests." Children generally made provision for the remaining parent. Typically, today males marry at twenty-two and females at 20.5 years and the wife has an average of two-plus children. The last child is born when the mother is twenty-six, and leaves home when the mother is forty-four and father forty-six. The parents can then expect to live together for some twenty additional years before the family is broken, generally by the death of the father. Typically, a block of this time will be in retirement. One out of ten retirees has a parent still living. Many persons will spend a third of their adult years in retirement, and some a third of their entire lives, since some persons retire already in their fifties. More than half of the people in the United States and Canada retire before sixty-five.

How do many people arrive at retirement?

People in retirement are faced with living on a reduced income, generally about half of what they made before retirement. They must learn how to substitute leisure activities for work and deal with the threats to health that accompany old age. It seems logical to assume that persons would plan carefully for retirement; unfortunately, this is not the case. Research has shown that those for whom retirement is likely to pose the most problems are least likely to plan for it, and those who attempt some planning do so in a desultory fashion. The majority arrive at the age of retirement without concrete, realistic plans. Many persons want to plan effectively for retirement, but they need help.

Productive extra days

Naturally, some persons will have more tomorrows than others, and the number has increased greatly since 1900. The potential keeps expanding; life expectancy in 1900 was forty-seven and today is seventy-four years. We have a great deal to say as to whether the extra days will be a bore or a bounty. It is quite certain that our later years will be most meaningful and useful if we realize early in life that we must plan to become the kind of older person we really want to be.

Life is intense and genuine, and its direction and goals must not be left to chance. However, we should not be thinking as much about lengthening the span of our years as about making this extra time a productive period.

In place of "retirement" think "retirement careers"

The word "retirement" is firmly embedded in our vocabulary with very sharp connotations, but in reality it should be considered a misnomer. It would be more accurate to speak of persons moving to retirement careers. We will continue to use the word *retirement,* but with the understanding that we don't believe people should ever be fully retired but should move to new retirement careers rather than "quitting."

Retirement careers are a time in life when we do not work full time for a living, when there is more free time and our decisions are not forced upon us by the time clock and fixed schedules. The family has been reared. We attempt to use free time in a positive way. Free time is not work in an economic sense, and leisure is much more than free time. Using leisure creatively has to be learned. In retirement careers we may spend a great deal of energy, sometimes as much as in working, but with a different motivation than in work or vocation.

Perspective for planning

Some persons think that it is useless to plan for a retirement career. They think the many changes which we cannot predict make planning a wasted effort. If our concept of planning is drawn in very fine lines rather than in broad strokes, this may be true.

One of the broad strokes to keep in mind when planning for retirement careers is flexibility. This should early become a hallmark of our lifestyle. Closed minds and unbending wills are not quality marks in character. Change is sure; unless we are able to compromise issues without compromising ourselves, obsolescence sets in early.

People are never too old to learn. Learning is not restricted to any particular period of life, nor must it occur in equal units on certain days of the week or at certain times of the day or in certain years. Learning implies that regardless of one's age, the individual's view of the world will shift. Learning is additive and cumulative. No living person ever completely matures. If we retain a reasonable measure of our mental resources, to our last breath we learn, we grow, we influence. We can't retire from life and we shouldn't want to.

Plan early

Retirement careers can and should be rich and full instead of a withdrawal from society. Productive retirement career living is based on wise planning. We should remember that God loves us for what we are and not for what we produce and give to others in a material way. However, productive retirement is more than killing time; it is redeeming the time with meaningful experiences not based on competition.

Early planning becomes the best insurance for a meaningful retirement career. A nursing instructor during her college education took a year to live "like eighty." She took ceramic and woodworking courses and followed up other interests which most of the time younger persons seem to be "too busy" to pursue.

It could almost be said that we should start planning for retirement at the very beginning of our working career. Savings and investment programs need to be planned to that end and thought must be given to the development of interest, skills, and mental outlooks that will make retirement years a rewarding time.
—William L. Mitchell in *Preparation for Retirement*
(U.S. Government Printing Office, 1968)

Dr. Arthur N. Schwartz, a psychologist on the faculty of University of Southern California, believes that counseling on retirement should be included in the curriculum of high school students. The White House Conference of 1971 recommended that since attitudes about aging are developed very young, elementary schools should provide some learning resources and experiences for young children regarding older persons. This can be done effectively by using suitable biographical materials about aging and citing experiences of North American pioneers.

Plan for what?

Financial planning should start early in life. It is not too early for children to learn how to use and manage money as soon as they may be able to handle an allowance. A child should learn to save, give, and spend. The late John D. Rockefeller II said that in his earlier days he received an allowance of forty-five cents per week of which he gave fifteen cents, saved fifteen cents, and spent the rest.

1. Where will I live at the different stages in retirement? How will the choices of where I live enhance my retirement activity?
2. How can I remain a contributing member of society?
3. How can I develop proper interpersonal relationships with my spouse twenty-four hours a day?
4. What can I expect to happen physically and mentally?
5. What are good activities—good hobbies—for leisure time, and how may I learn to use leisure better?
6. How can I continue to build friendships?
7. How can I continue my education in formal or informal ways?
8. Where can I go for help with different kinds of problems?
9. How can I better prepare to cope with reality—stress, rackets, swindles?

Not all of these questions can be projected adequately in earlier life. But if we think through the issues and do some careful planning, we are in a much stronger position when we reach the realities.

Plan to master leisure time

In 1973 I asked a group of older persons to give a written answer to this question: "As a result of your retirement experience what single bit of counsel would you give to middle-aged persons?" Out of some sixty responses more than two thirds firmly suggested the importance of developing hobbies. It is difficult to use greatly increased free time in a meaningful way if we have had no positive experience in using leisure throughout life, from earlier years to retirement.

Leisure activities may be defined as activities in which a person might indulge of his own free will, either to rest, to amuse himself, to add to his knowledge or to improve his skills without increasing his earning power or to maintain his voluntary participation in the life of the community. The definition includes the things a person is constrained to do to earn money, maintain his health, or keep house. It excludes sleeping, eating, dressing, cooking, cleaning, and travel to and from work.
—Harold Lehman in *In Praise of Leisure* (Herald Press, 1974)

What makes a good hobby?*

A good hobby must be one you enjoy, not one that somebody else suggests you ought to enjoy. An excellent hobby for one person may be wrong for another.

A good hobby should be something worth doing and should accomplish the following:

1. **Help you relax and put your problems in the background for the time being.**
2. **Give real satisfaction in the activity itself.**
3. **Be more than a mere time-waster.**
4. **Produce something worth producing, either tangible or intangible.**
5. **Increase your knowledge and skills.**
6. **Cost no more than you can afford; it may even produce revenue.**

Collecting offers a great field for developing a hobby. The collector may save anything from precious jewelry to pocket matchbooks. Some collectors' items emphasize antiquity, some beauty, some rarity, some utility, and some just the collector's personal interest.

Developing skills may be a fine hobby. Many people train themselves in skills outside their business and professional lines. Doctors, lawyers, and statesmen, for example, paint, invent mechanical gadgets, play musical instruments, or study ancient history.

Making things is often a satisfying hobby, provided there is a real use for what is made. Craftsmanship can be developed in wood, metal, leather, plastics, or other materials.

Among the best hobbies is service to others. This can be personal in nature, as was the case with the retired man who loved to tinker with things that needed repair and who helped neighbors with repair jobs around their homes.

Service is needed by many organizations—churches, neighborhood houses, voluntary health agencies, and social service organizations. This may be almost anything from stuffing en-

---

*This section is reprinted from *More Life for Your Years* (August 1971), copyright 1971, American Medical Society.

velopes for an education or fund-raising campaign to preparing meals or serving refreshments.

An important opportunity for service exists in hospitals, outpatient medical services, public health clinics, and immunizing stations. Here the shortage of trained and practical nurses can be eased by nurses' aides, Gray Ladies, and clerical volunteers.

A hobby cannot be picked up overnight. It should be the logical outcome of developing interests which may be expanded when there is leisure time during vacations or when retired. A good hobby can be an emotional lifesaver.

A good hobby is not antisocial

Hobbies are important because of what they bring to the individual and in many cases as spin-off benefits to society. A good hobby can never be antisocial. The purpose for following a hobby, however, is defeated if we feel that every leisure-time pursuit must be of direct benefit to society. Society benefits if an individual becomes a better person through wholesome leisure-time pursuits.

INVOLVEMENT:
Identifying plants in Parson's Swamp Woods

S. W. Witmer spent the better part of 1979 identifying the plant life in a new park that has become a nature classroom for the residents of Goshen, Indiana.

At age ninety, Dr. Witmer undertook the project of marking the various shrubs, plants, and trees in Parson's Swamp Woods. He found new and rare plant life in the area, in addition to about sixty different kinds of trees, forty different kinds of shrubs, and 230 different kinds of wildflowers. Most of these, he said in a story by Jeff Edwards in the local newspaper, *The Goshen News,* he knew from memory. "But when you get older, the memory can play tricks on you."

There were no trees within the park Dr. Witmer could not identify, but he had to check out some of the wildflowers. A hedge parsley plant stumped him, and he said he had never seen the plant before. "It's rare in Indiana." He found the rare flowering rush plant, the glossy buck horn, and three silver berry shrubs in the park.

The popular names of the plants, their scientific names, and pictures were painted on identifying markers by Goshen artist Gloria Leer. Dr. Witmer rode his bicycle to the park most days from April to late fall. His investment in identifying the plant life will be viewed by schoolchildren and park visitors for years to come. "His knowledge will help to make Parson's Swamp Woods one of Goshen's greatest assets," concluded Jeff Edwards. Dr. Witmer came to the Goshen College campus in 1909, first as a student and later as professor of biology.

STARTERS

1
What do you want to be doing a month after you retire from your regular job? Have an older person, who to you has successfully made the transition, advise you. Check out some of the books on the subject.

2
A recently retired person you know seems not too sure of what to make of his or her new freedom. Seek an opportunity to listen. Listen. The words may mask the real feelings, leaving out more than is said. Listen. What hints does the person give about a better road ahead—with a little encouragement from a friend?

3
How do your parents or grandparents embody a creative approach to retirement careers? You're more than likely to follow in their steps—unless you fail to plan. What wisdom are they waiting to pass on to you?

4
What would you do if you didn't have to work to make ends meet? Now is the time to plan for that eventuality. Take stock of your interests and make a list of possible retirement career options—a one-, five-, ten-, twenty-, and forty-year plan.

5
How can you help your spouse or close friend prepare for a creative retirement career?

6
When did you last hear your pastor preach a sermon on full living after sixty-five? Pertinent Scriptures would include Zechariah 8:1-6; James 1:27; Galatians 6:2; 1 Samuel 12:1-5; Ephesians 4:11-16; Psalm 71:17, 18; John 19:25-27; and Psalm 92:12-15. Use a concordance to locate more. Share your findings.

7
Many older persons spend more time in Bible reading and prayer. Practice the discipline of a devotional life and expect deeper meaning in it in later years. On a few occasions in your life take the opportunity for an extended reflective retreat.

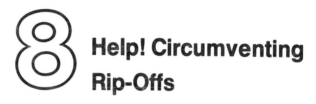

Help! Circumventing Rip-Offs

There is common decency among most North Americans today, but there is also an upsurge of persons scheming to make money through fraudulent and illegitimate means. Street crimes, white-collar crimes, rip-offs, huckster bargains, and medical quacks are common. Rip-offs include any form of financial exploitation. The elderly, many of whom live at or below the poverty level, and particularly elderly women who live alone, are prime targets. Middle-aged persons should be wise to the ways of con artists and be advocates for the safety and protection of more vulnerable persons.

State of the times

In a TV interview June 24, 1976, Archibald McLeish, 83, American poet and administrator, was asked by Bill Moyers what he thought was the greatest American problem of our time. McLeish answered that to him it is the loss of individual respect for the common good—the welfare of the community. He said that love has given way to material gain regardless of means, accompanied with the thirst for personal power with personal arrogance.

At this point we will not philosophize on the sociology, economics, psychology, or theology of causes and cures, but rather will offer some suggestions by which the elderly and their younger advocates may help themselves to become less vulnerable.

Many fraud peddlers use fear tactics in some form or another: "Your furnace is about to blow up." "Your roof is about to collapse." "Your car transmission is about to crack up and you might get caught on a busy highway." "You don't hear as well as you once did (most people don't) and your nerve fibers need restimulating through a special hearing aid." Pictures may be shown of elderly persons trapped in flaming buildings as the huckster demonstrates an overpriced fire-alarm system. Sometimes our fears, excitement, loneliness, or other emotions obscure our common sense and judgment. You can always expect a catch in something that sounds too good to be true. A good rule is not to buy when you are emotionally charged. Sleep on it and never buy anything out of fear. Deal only with reputable business people.

Consumers' guide

A wallet-size *Consumers' Guide* issued by the Province of Ontario is available through the Consumer Protection Bureau, 555 Yonge Street, Toronto, Ontario, M4Y 1Y7. A similar guide, *Consumer Guide for Older People,* is offered by the Superintendent of Documents, U.S. Government Printing Office, Washington, D.C., 20402.

Password 'caution'*

To protect yourself from rip-offs, consider the following cautions:

1. Signing your name. Before you sign a contract or an agreement, ask yourself:

Do I understand everything it says?

Do I agree with everything it says?

Are all the promises and guarantees in writing?

If your answer is "NO" to any question, DON'T SIGN. Check with your lawyer or someone experienced with the law of contracts.

---

*This section is reprinted from the *Ontario Guide for Senior Citizens.*

2. Buying by mail or at the door. Don't fall for gimmicks, free gifts, an easy way to make money at home, a bargain home in the sun, a "get-rich-quick" scheme, or payment for referring your friends. Don't be rushed into making an instant decision without careful thought. Some door-to-door sales can be canceled by registered mail within two days, but it is always wiser to do your thinking before you buy.

3. Buying on credit. Don't be fooled by talk of low payments or easy credit. The law requires all the following items to be filled in on your purchase contract:

> Cash price
> Down payment
> Total finance charges
> Annual percentage rate (interest rate)
> Amount of each payment
> Total number of payments

If there are any blank spaces, DON'T SIGN, DON'T BUY. Don't be pressured into buying on credit rather than paying cash.

4. Inspectors who come to your home. Don't let servicemen, telephone inspectors, or repairmen into your home unless you see clear identification from the company they represent. Don't hesitate to refuse admittance until you have telephoned the company they claim to represent.

Particularly guard against phony bank inspectors. No bank will call you to take money out of your account to help them catch a supposed thief. NEVER! Call the police and bank immediately and do not withdraw money from your bank.

5. Home repairs. Remember that repairs to your home are a major expenditure. Don't rush into a decision. Be suspicious of door-to-door salesmen offering deals on paving, chimney repairs, roofing, or siding. Get other estimates; check their reputation. If you have to sign a large contract, read it all! Consult your lawyer if you are unsure of the contract.

6. Health care. Always check with your doctor or medical officer of health before you buy a health cure or join a health club. Some programs may actually turn out to be injurious to your health. Concerning hearing aids and glasses, consult your family doctor who will probably refer you to a specialist to determine whether glasses or a hearing aid will help your particular type of sight or hearing problem. Buy only from reputable dealers who will provide correct fittings.

7. Social clubs. Before you sign a contract with a social club or a dance studio, be sure you know the total cost. Check with your information sources about the reputation of the club. Be wary of vacations that promise you a social whirl for just a few dollars. Remember, if you want companionship, there are many excellent Senior Citizens Clubs, Elderly Persons Centers, adult education programs, community recreation centers and libraries, with programs you will enjoy.

8. Some special tips. Don't be afraid to say no. Don't be high-pressured into buying something you don't want or need, or making a snap decision.

Always check on a seller. Ask your friends and the information sources listed here. The only companies who object to this are the ones who are trying to take advantage of you.

You must make up your own mind. If it sounds too good to be true, it probably is. But if you are having trouble deciding and need advice, ASK.

When you buy, ask for a receipt and read it through carefully. Make sure all promises and guarantees are in writing.

Talk with your bank manager if you are going into your savings for a business deal or a large purchase.

If you need help and are unsure of the government department concerned, contact your local elected representative who will answer your questions or direct you to the agency involved.

To foil the purse-snatcher

Information with the film, *Senior Power and How to Use It* (available through Motorola Teleprograms, Inc., 4825 N. Scott

Street, Schiller Park, IL 60176), suggests the following methods
for coping with different kinds of exploitation:

1. *Use a whistle.* A whistle is loud and clear.
You're not likely to "clam up" from fear. You don't have to
remember to say anything special. If you are accosted,
blow it! A standard plastic police whistle is safest.

2. *Sit down.* Those "good old bones" don't like bounc-
ing off the sidewalk. If it looks like you're in for a lot of
shoving and pushing, take the sting out of it by sitting
down yourself. Then wrap one arm about your head for
protection and keep blowing that whistle! Most purse-
snatchers attack "on the run"—and they'll keep on running.

3. *Why carry a purse?* Leave all your extra money in a
safe place (large sums of money should remain in your
checking or savings account). Carry only the money you
need for each day (plus change for emergency phone calls
and enough for an emergency taxi fare). Find a special
place to carry money without a wallet or purse.

Coping with armed robbery

Never argue with a gun. Robbers are nervous, often being
under the influence of narcotics. Try to stay calm and pleasant.
Make no quick arm movements (he might think you've got a
gun, too). You're just as dead if you're killed by a knife, club, or
heavy pipe. Don't argue with them either. Husbands and wives
should discuss the possibility of robbery. Don't expect "dad" to
spring into action. Protect your life and your spouse's life by
staying cool in the face of robbery. Hand over the money de-
manded without arguing or trying to use delaying tactics.

Home security

Many law enforcement agencies will make a "home security
survey" for you. Here are some points to consider:

1. *Doors.* A dead-bolt lock offers good protection (if
it's on a solid door). Install a "fish-eye" or other viewing
device. Cheap door chains won't protect you. Don't "hide"
a key outside, crooks can always find them. Make sure
there is no glass (French door, or adjacent window) within
reach of the door lock.

2. *Windows.* **Use a locking device, a jam lock if you want to keep the window slightly open. Bedroom windows should not have bars as they would prevent escape from fire.**

3. *Lights and sounds.* **Leave lights on in logical locations in your home. Install a timer device to switch them on and off when you're away. (Use low-wattage light bulbs to conserve energy.) Turn your radio to a talk show when you are out.**

4. *Single women.* **Do not put your first name on the mail box or in the telephone book. Use last name only or use initials with last name.**

Real estate swindles

Thousands of persons each year are "taken" in real estate swindles. Older persons who may wish to move to the Sun Belt are especially vulnerable.*

Have you been tempted by colorful brochures inviting you to own property in a development in a sunny climate? Before you invest in a "dream" location, be sure you know what you are getting for your money. Get the answers to these questions at the very least:

1. Is the real estate developer's report to the state's real estate commission available? Get a copy if you can and read it carefully.

2. Does the salesman have any actual photographs of land to contrast with the artist's concept of what the property might someday resemble?

3. Who drew the map of the real estate development? Does it make the property appear to be more accessible and closer to vital services and conveniences than is the fact?

4. Does the contract state exactly what improvements will be installed—and when?

5. Are distances described as "minutes away" or in miles over travelable roads?

6. Does the contract contain a non-acceleration clause which prevents taking of title and deed before it suits the

---

*The following advice is from an article, "Your Place in the Sun—Know What You Are Buying," in *More Life for Your Years,* (August 1973), copyright 1973, American Medical Association.

developer's convenience or his ability to release his mortgage or
get subdivision approval?

7. If a money refund is assurance given, is it necessary to
travel all the way to the property to get it?

8. Have you really read the purchase contract—not just the
bold type that the seller would like to have you read, but the fine
print containing information presented in the dullest possible
way?

Give wisely and well

On numerous occasions we are asked to make contributions
for various causes, many worthwhile. This is particularly true,
since the starving and undernourished millions throughout the
world can so vividly come to our attention through television
and other media. Persons should give to community enterprises
which depend on citizen support, as well as to church agencies.
With the plethora of opportunities, older persons with limited
resources can rightly be more selective in their giving.

Even the church must be careful in its appraisals, because in
many cases unscrupulous predators use the church and its good
graces for immoral purposes. A missions administrator told of a
special appeal to American church members: "A recent radio
broadcast made a hard sell appeal for large contributions ($1,000
was suggested) for starving people in Dhamtari, India. As a
former resident in Dhamtari, I am aware that the 'doctor' who
receives the funds has less formal education than a registered
nurse."

The case was investigated by an Indian church leader who
said, "We checked on the feeding program Dr. Silas had and
found he had fifty to 100 beggars for a one-day feeding program,
and that was the day he apparently took the picture which Dr.
Douglas had produced in his magazine. At this site we did not
see any feeding shack or ongoing arrangements."

How can charitable rip-offs be avoided?

In general, our charitable dollars should go to causes close
at hand which can be well identified. Our local churches
generally receive gifts for many causes worldwide, as well as at
home. Other community causes worthy of support can easily be

checked. Your family banker, your lawyer, and friends with broad financial experience can be helpful.

The National Information Bureau has established these "Basic Standards in Philanthropy":

Philanthropic organizations have a high degree of responsibility because of the public trusteeship involved. Compliance with the following standards, with reasonable evidence supplied on request, is considered essential for approval by the NIB:

1. *Board.* An active and responsible governing body, serving without compensation, holding regular meetings, and with effective administrative control.

2. *Purpose.* A legitimate purpose with no avoidable duplication of the work of other sound organizations.

3. *Program.* Reasonable management efficiency with adequate material and personnel resources to carry on its stated program together with reasonable administration and fund-raising expense.

4. *Cooperation.* Consultation and cooperation with established agencies in the same and related fields.

5. *Ethical promotion.* Ethical methods of publicity, promotion, and solicitation of funds.

6. *Fund-raising practice.*
   a. No payment of commissions for fund raising.
   b. No mailing of unordered tickets or merchandise with a request for money in return.
   c. No general telephone solicitation of the public.
   d. No use of identified government employees in solicitation of the public.

7. *Audit.* Annual audit employing the Uniform Accounting Standards and prepared by an independent certified public accountant, showing all Support/Revenue and Expenses in reasonable detail. New organizations should provide an independent certified public accountant's statement that a proper financial system has been installed.

8. *Budget.* Detailed annual budget, consistent with the Uniform Accounting Standards employed in the audit report, translating program plans into financial terms.

Unordered merchandise

The Federal Trade Commission (FTC Buyers Guide No. 2) says, "There are only two kinds of merchandise which can be sent legally through the mails to a person without his consent or agreement:

"*1. Free samples which are clearly and plainly marked as such.*

"*2. Merchandise mailed by a charitable organization asking for contributions.*

"In either of the above cases you can consider the merchandise as a gift if you like. Should you receive unordered merchandise of any kind, take it as a gift, you do not have to pay for it and it is illegal for the person or firm sending it to you to dun you for it or send you a bill."

Social Security check safety

An avalanche of stealing Social Security checks, or mugging the client after cashing the check, prompted the federal government to arrange to send Social Security checks directly to the client's bank accounts if they so desired. The individual accounts are credited regularly without delay and there is no danger of check delay, loss, or theft. Arrangements can easily be made through your local banks at your initiative.

Many banks encourage banking by mail for your other accounts also. Postage is paid by the bank as you send in your checks and as they report to you. This saves you the inconvenience of going to the bank and standing in line. The bank can handle mail accounts leisurely and accurately with special personnel. Many banks accommodate older citizens by not making bank or personal check charges. In the course of a year, this is an appreciable savings to older citizens.

Making a will

Making a will is one of the most important things we can do. However, many do not take this obligation seriously.

Making a will does not prevent you from beginning to liquidate your estate while you are alive if you can afford it. Many are too cautious in this area. There can be great joy in seeing your gifts become fruitful. One wag stated: "Do your givin' while you're livin' so you're knowin' where it's goin'!"

It is particularly important for wives to insist on a will. Typically, the wife will live eight years in widowhood; there are four times more widows than widowers. Most women are not familiar with family finances. This can easily be remedied. Making a will is a joint responsibility to which both husband and wife should give high priority. Singles on their own, too, should have a will.

If you do not make a will, your estate will be distributed according to the laws of the state in which you reside. Failure to make a will almost invariably results in significantly increasing settlement costs and taxes, and also results in unnecessary delays in the distribution of your estate.

How much of your estate should your children share?

In the early twentieth century few young people went to high school. They usually worked at home without remuneration until they were twenty-one. If they did work out for wages, the money generally went to the parents until the child was "of age." Consequently, a child contributed seven or eight years of effort to the family enterprise. This often made it possible for parents to buy a home or to pay off the mortgage on the farm.

Today the situation has changed a great deal. A high school education is considered an inherent right, and school attendance is required for a specific number of years. Frequently the child goes on to college and parents have further financial obligations. If children don't complete college and find jobs on their own, within a decade or less they may earn more than the parents did even at their peak of earning. In over 50 percent of the cases, young married partners will both work and can soon build up a substantial earning base.

This pattern is not true in all cases, but where it is, most children do not need financial aid at the time of the parents' death. The children's special needs should have been met by parents earlier when financial stress is more apt to come. Accordingly, it is appropriate for parents to make wills which leave most of their assets to institutions—chiefly religious, but also secular—to which they were not able earlier to contribute fully and which may depend entirely on the good graces of individual charity.

INVOLVEMENT: How to make your money outlive you

We cannot make plans for every eventuality which may come in later years, however, plan we must. We should make some "dry runs" to test ourselves on living on half our regular income. We need the experience of actually cutting back in expenditures to see where and how this can be done without creating too much trauma. That's one way to prepare for secure—and rewarding—retirement years.

John H. Rudy is general manager of financial services of Mennonite Mutual Aid, Goshen, Indiana. He has had many years of experience in business, first as an engineer for RCA and for more than fifteen years with the Mennonite Foundation. He finds many avenues to help persons think through wise management of their resources. We are happy to share some of his insights here.

FINANCIAL PLANNING
By John H. Rudy

"I'm outliving my money. The cost of living is rising faster than my Social Security and pension benefits. My savings are shrinking. I can't go anywhere or do anything. I can't give as much. Shuffleboard isn't enough. Retirement isn't all it's cracked up to be."

That's the unfortunate dilemma of many retired people. Retirement looked so exciting. They had so many things they wanted to do. There were so many places they could be helpful. Now they have the time. They enjoy good health. But there isn't enough money.

Too many people retire and then make the discovery that they are receiving only half of their pre-retirement income. There's a horrible shock because most people need retirement income of nearly 80 percent of their working income just to support their pre-retirement standards of living.

The problem is simply this: Many people don't start early enough to plan for retirement. On the threshold of retiring they ask, "Now, what can I do to assure myself a good retirement income?" Usually it's too late. The best time to plan for your retirement is now. The earlier the better. Even people in their thirties and forties should begin preparing financially for retirement.

"How much will I need in retirement?" That's a good question. And it's a hard question. It depends upon so many things:

inflation, your health, your lifestyle, where you live.

Inflation will probably continue to be a real bugaboo. It will make retirement planning more difficult. Constant increases in the cost of living can be devastating. You'll need more money every year after the paychecks stop. For example, you may decide you can retire on $10,000 a year. But in ten years, at an inflation rate of just 7 percent per year, you will need almost $20,000 per year to support the same lifestyle. That's downright scary.

Longevity may make planning still more difficult. Retirement may be longer than you expected. Average life expectancies are increasing. A woman age sixty-five will live an average of eighteen additional years. A man sixty-five will live fourteen more years. That's a long time to provide income.

On the income side of retirement, you may be expecting too much from Social Security. Or, you may think your pension plan will take good care of you. The truth is that you may need more than Social Security and pension benefits together will provide. You will need some personal savings. Too many people consider saving obsolete.

So, maybe the watchword for retirement is planning. Start now. Put aside what you can for retirement. Don't let go of your accumulated resources too soon. Sure, give what you can to your children. Give generously to the church and other charitable organizations. But be concerned about yourself. Retain plenty for retirement. Then plan final disposition through your will.

Now, as you proceed with your financial planning for retirement, try to identify and project the principal sources of your retirement income:

1. Retirement job. You probably won't want a rocking chair. And you'll soon get your fill of fishing and golf. You may want to work as long as you can, after sixty-five, if you're enjoying good health. You'll need some useful activity. Maybe it's voluntary service. But maybe you'll need to accept whatever annual earned income is allowed by Social Security, without losing any benefits. Unearned income such as pension benefits, rents, dividends and interest will not affect your Social Security payments.

2. Social Security. Retirement benefits from Social Security were never meant to provide all your retirement needs. In fact, you may find that your Social Security checks are meeting only half your needs. However, there is some good news: Your Social Security payments are expected to increase with inflation. Better check with your local Social Security office to determine what benefits you have earned.

3. Pension plans. You may be fortunate enough to be participating in a company retirement plan which will supplement your Social Security benefits. As a self-employed person you may be contributing money into a Keogh Plan. If you are not in any retirement plan, you should consider putting tax-deferred money into an Individual Retirement Account (IRA) or annuity. Check periodically to determine what retirement benefits you can expect from your pension plan.

4. Savings. Don't rely completely on Social Security and pension plans. Try to accumulate some savings and invest them wisely. Maybe it's equity in your house. Or farmland. Or stocks and bonds. Savings accounts and certificates of deposit have their place. In retirement you will be more concerned about good income and safety of principal. If you can find some safe hedges against inflation, so much the better.

5. Charitable life income plans. You can contribute cash or property to a gift annuity or charitable remainder trust. In addition to participating in church causes, you receive income as long as you live. Some plans provide fixed payments. In other plans the payments vary from year to year. You may achieve some significant tax savings.

Trying to provide adequate income for your retirement is an important element of your planning. But that's not all. There are other important matters which ought to be part of your planning:

1. Adopt an appropriate lifestyle. You may not have enough income to support a lavish standard of living during retirement.

But even if you did, a moderate lifestyle seems more responsible. Beyond the usual income constraints, there are some good reasons for enjoying life within reason: To conserve resources. To be a good steward. To reduce waste. To obey biblical injunctions.

2. Keep your will up to date. Try to provide for the legitimate needs of your children. Include as much as possible for the work of the church. Take advantage of tax-saving methods. Choose a good executor to settle your estate. Provide a guardian for any minor children. There are a number of changes which may necessitate that your lawyer revise your will: when the size of your estate increases or decreases, when you move from one state to another, when the needs of your children diminish, when you want to designate more for charity, when you need to name a new executor, when tax laws change.

3. Make lifetime gifts to your children. The best time to help your children is when they need it the most, when they're young, not when you pass away and they receive their inheritances at age fifty by way of your will. If you have some resources which you won't need for your retirement, try to make some gifts now. There are ways to transfer cash and property without paying Federal Gift Tax. Lifetime gifts sometimes provide savings in estate and inheritance taxes.

4. Give generously to charitable organizations. Congregations, church institutions, and other charitable organizations need your help now. You can participate by making outright gifts. Or you can give cash or property and retain lifetime income. You may be able to achieve some significant savings in income, estate, and inheritance taxes. A good counselor can help you choose the gift methods which best achieve your objectives.

5. Reinforce your buyer resistance. Someone is always trying to relieve you of your worldly possessions. There are all kinds of schemes, ways to make a killing, products to make life more comfortable. They sound so good. Beware. Especially as you grow older, you need to strengthen your defenses. Older people

are sometimes easy prey for the unscrupulous. Too many have
lost their life savings.

6. Appraise your needs for insurance. It is often said that insurance is sold and not bought. How much life insurance do you
need? Health insurance? Automobile insurance? Liability insurance? Don't buy too much insurance. But be sure you have
adequate protection. Find yourself an insurance counselor you
can trust.

7. Make sure you have adequate liquidity. It's possible to be
wealthy without having adequate income. You can have everything tied up in land or a closely held business which doesn't
yield much steady income. As you approach retirement you will
want to rearrange your assets to provide greater income and
easier access to principal.

8. Get acquainted with death tax implications. The federal
government imposes an estate tax on the transfer of assets at
death. Many states have inheritance taxes. The more you are
worth at death the higher these taxes will be. You may need to do
some comprehensive estate planning. In fact, more and more
people need estate planning, especially farmers and business
persons. Try to find a competent and objective estate planner,
not one who is just trying to sell you something.

9. Examine the complications of joint ownership. Many husbands and wives own property in joint tenancy with rights of sur-
vivorship. When one spouse dies the other spouse has sole
ownership of the entire property. This method of ownership has
some advantages. But it can create some problems for you,
particularly if you have a large estate. Federal Estate Tax may be
higher than necessary. Rearrangement of ownership may be
advisable. Perhaps some property should be in your name. Other
property might be put in your spouse's name. Hopefully, you can
accomplish this without incurring Federal Gift Tax. You should
stay close to good legal and tax counsel.

10. Utilize helpful government programs. Social Security provides more than retirement benefits. For example, there are survivors and disability benefits. At age sixty-five you are entitled to medical and hospital benefits under Medicare. Federal Income Tax regulations provide some tax relief to persons age sixty-five and older. After age fifty-five you can avoid capital gains tax on sale of a residence.

11. Give someone a power of attorney. So many older people are no longer able to cash their checks, pay their bills, and handle their financial affairs. They're considered incompetent. The family may need to petition the court for powers to handle the financial matters of an incompetent father or mother. A much better way would be for you to have your lawyer prepare a power of attorney for you to sign. A son or daughter could be given the authority to handle your affairs when you are no longer able.

12. Tell your family where everything is located. You may have your important papers scattered all over the place: deeds, stock certificates, bonds, insurance policies, tax returns, birth certificates, etc. Why not keep your children informed on the location of everything. Consider putting everything on paper: the location of your will, important papers, burial lots, bank accounts, safe-deposit box, etc. Outline any funeral instructions. Then give copies to your children.

13. Seek competent financial and legal counsel. Planning for the future, particularly retirement, can be bewildering. It's becoming more complex all the time. Investments, insurance, estate planning, wills, Social Security, pension plans—the list goes on and on. You need a good lawyer. You may need to seek the guidance of tax accountants, insurance agents, investment managers, and other knowledgeable persons whom you can trust. And you can benefit from the counsel of your church community.

Retirement can be one of the most enjoyable and rewarding periods of your life. But you'll need adequate income, and you'll need to keep your financial house in order. That will take some very careful planning, starting now.

STARTERS

1

You know the saying about locking the stable door after the horse has been stolen. See that the older persons you know understand and have available services for their protection.

2

Somebody close to you or in your group experiences some form of rip-off. What do you do? What instances do you recall in which the offender has been dealt with redemptively and has changed his ways? Accentuate the positive and support efforts toward aiding the victim and reconciling the offender.

3

You've made your will. It's properly updated, too. When have you had such a sense of deep satisfaction in the disposition of your resources? Congratulations!

4

What models of philanthropy are you showing your children?

5

Are you financially prepared to begin retirement when that time comes? Or should you take advantage of a preparing-for-retirement seminar or adult class at your local college or church?

6

Contrary to what we might sometimes be tempted to believe, there are many honest, well-meaning folk around. Including you! Let there be "salt and light" at work in your community.

7

Oh, oh, you're the victim of a rip-off. Be ready to receive help. Don't blame yourself unduly. In some circumstances a counselor should be sought to help us overcome feelings of fear and anger. Take stock of the blessings around you. Do a good turn for someone. You've been "hurt," but you're still the master and ultimate winner.

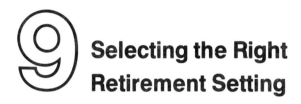

Selecting the Right Retirement Setting

By far the majority of persons will continue to live in retirement just as they did prior to retirement—independently in their own homes. Those with medical, nutritional, or other needs will continue to live independently in their own homes, too, given a wise and alert community which provides support services.

Some persons will choose to live in apartments, courts, retirement homes, or condominiums, perhaps as part of a retirement community. These options, like one's own home, provide for independent living. Some persons will graduate to a small suite in a building complex, such as an efficiency apartment. Here some or all meals may be furnished in a central dining room with some assisted living services available, such as transportation, health services, food preparation, purchasing services, and room care.

Other persons will live with family members. Some will need the services of a nursing or convalescent home. Many will spend their last days in a hospital or hospice.

Whatever the arrangement, retirement living will have been most rewarding if persons have had the opportunity to choose the right living option for them at the right time. Before looking more closely at the various options, we should recognize some of the helpful principles of retirement living exemplified by the Old Order Amish of North America.

Retire like the Amish?

The Amish are farmers or follow related careers which

allow them to live in the local Amish church community. They operate their farms with horses, which they also use for transportation. The Amish do not use electricity, tractors, automobiles, telephones, or other worldly gadgets. Their lifestyle is simple. Independently or as a brotherhood, they are able to meet their needs for food, clothing, shelter, transportation, education, recreation, religious training, and security, reasonably free from worldly dictates.

Accordingly, the retirement practices of the Amish remain those of rural people who continue to live close to the soil. There is much we could learn from the Amish about the basic ingredients for meaningful retirement living.

Amish retirement practices. To compile the following list of Amish retirement practices, I have drawn extensively from the section entitled "Old Folks" in the book *Children in Amish Society* by John A. Hostetler and Gertrude E. Huntington. I also visited a number of Amish homes, and talked with other persons who were formerly Amish.

1. The chronological age for retirement is not rigidly fixed. It may commonly be anywhere between fifty and seventy. The health, inclination of the individual, and family needs are important factors.

2. Retirement is both voluntary and gradual. The retiree determines the amount and kind of work he wishes to do and the time schedule.

3. Work expectations are reduced without losing prestige. It is assumed that older people will work fewer hours and at less strenuous tasks, but this does not cause them to lose status. It is not a question of full-time labor or doing nothing. Health permitting, each will be engaged in meaningful activity.

4. Income is seldom a serious problem. There is generally economic sufficiency without dependence on the federal government for Social Security or on other governmental agencies for aid. Life earnings, rental income from a farm, carpentry, or other part-time work provides sufficient income.

5. Private housing is provided. A separate house for the grandparents is built near their old home, allowing for independence without sacrificing intergenerational family involvement.

6. Continuity of care is provided. With the grandparents living near the children, special care can be given as needed. This is considered as a normal arrangement by both generations.

7. There is free contact and interaction with all age-groups. Family, relatives, and friends provide multigenerational contacts and generally there is no fear of loneliness.

8. Grandparents, parents, and children work together at common tasks. They learn from each other; their goals are strengthened through discussion and personal interaction.

9. Leisure-time activities are abundant and meaningful. Examples include carpentry, caring for livestock, gardening, flower culture, quiltings, visiting friends (including the sick and the bereaved), attending funerals, visitations over wide areas (including distant states) which involve other forms of transportation than the horse and buggy, weddings, the weekly auction, and farm sales.

10. Transportation is always available. Retirees have their own horse and buggy and continue to travel to the points they customarily covered in the past. There is no fear of losing a driver's license!

11. The slow rate of change makes for strong community ties. Older people are assured of meaningful social participation and minimal trauma or frustration which comes from the "trampling" of traditions.

12. Prestige seems to increase with age. Older men and women keep their rights to a formal vote in all church and school matters. Participation in church and community activities continue naturally. There is no such thing as retirement from certain activities. For instance, church offices, such as bishop, preacher, and deacon, continue for life since ordination is a lifetime commitment.

13. Old-fashioned ways are perpetuated and younger people look to the elders for direction. Young farmers, for instance, will ask their fathers about farming methods, and mothers are available for advice on raising children. This does not mean that every bit of advice is accepted, but at least the parent is recognized and his or her views are solicited and respected.

14. There is a continued participation in mutual aid and sharing (barn raisings, for example). Financial aid by parents and

grandparents is a common financial expectation for younger persons who may have special needs for buying a farm or for other business ventures. Often interest is not charged, or the rate is low.

15. There is an abiding interest in the well-being of others. This is often expressed beyond the primary group and includes a concern for non-Amish neighbors. The Amish support the Mennonite Central Committee's worldwide mission of relief and service.

16. Institutional homes for the aging are generally not needed. The sick and the elderly are a concern of all. The ill are talked about and visited, and small gifts such as food and other tokens of good will are taken to them. In this way, regardless of their physical condition, they have a sense of belonging and continued acceptance. The family next door, generally a son or daughter and spouse, is always available.

17. Education for retirement is built-in. There is little need for additional education in the vocational field as the Amish grow older. As long as the Amish are small in numbers and can remain essentially a rural people, continuing education to meet job changes or for promotional purposes in "getting ahead" is not needed. Continuing education for the Amish way of life comes as nature continues to teach those who love the soil and respect the Creator as well as the creation. The Amish also have a way of getting the benefits of the education of others in such areas as medicine, agronomy, animal husbandry, transportation, merchandising, rural science, and industry. Education for retirement is built into the system because the retiree knows clearly what he is going to do when he becomes elderly: he is going to continue the things he has always done but on a lesser scale and with less responsibility.

18. Health and good nutrition are sustained. Medical and dental aid is generally available in the rural towns which serve the Amish, as are hospitals and other health agencies which serve the kind of rural communities in which the Amish settle. Good food is always in abundance and air pollution is at a minimum. Hard physical labor and exercise late into life keep the body active. Relatives and friends keep loneliness at a low level and generally the elderly do not have mental health problems.

19. Advocacy is supplied. Elderly Amish have little need for non-Amish advocates to plead their causes as do many other elderly citizens. They do not seek or need counsel regarding their rights: how to get financial aid, Medicare, Medicaid, food stamps, or housing. These services are either not needed or are supplied by relatives and friends. In cases which may require some political activity, the kindly intercession of "outsiders" is generally a tribute to the common decency of the Amish as seen by their neighbors and other interested citizens. The resources of persons, funds, and talent which took the Amish case on education to the Supreme Court of the United States is a dramatic example.

20. Sickness has no stigma. John A. Hostetler in *Amish Life* says, "Sickness is a socially approved form of deviation in Amish life; as in the great society the sick role is increasingly sanctioned as one alternative in the problem of adjustment." Thus a person may become sick and find this to be an advantageous position where he is visited much and concern is expressed from many different areas.

21. Strong religious teaching and practice build a lifelong faith. Children are under a strong religious influence from their birth. A simple Christian faith results which sustains the elderly to the end. All are taught that this life is but the passageway to life eternal. Death is the threshold over which one passes to something far better than one could even imagine. Death is a reminder to those left behind that there is "no abiding city here" and life is preparatio 1 for death.

22. There is integrity rather than despair in the final stages of life. Death is humanized and generally takes place in the individual's own home with family and friends nearby. There are no fears of frustrations about spending money which would make the funeral "respectable" or one which cannot be afforded. Simple burial practices are common to all. The coffin is a plain varnished pine box made by a local Amish carpenter, the hearse a one-horse spring wagon. The body may or may not be embalmed and the costs of the undertaker's services are low.

Emulate the Amish? Does this mean we should all try to follow the exact pattern of the Amish? Hardly. Large populations cannot be sustained by a basically rural economy. It would be presumptuous to assume that a majority of our North American population should become "dirt" farmers. If all farming operations in North America were energized by live horsepower we might not be experiencing the present energy crisis. However, a sufficient number of animals needed to supply power for all farming operations would use many acres of productive land which could not be spared for the production of human food and fiber and might create another kind of crisis.

In the second place, many of us would not want to follow the simple lifestyle of the Amish. We wouldn't be willing to give up automobiles, tractors, electrical appliances, carpets and draperies, telephones, insurance, convenience foods, television and radio, modern clothes, and various forms of entertainment. We consider education above the elementary school, reading materials, and church programs of outreach (such as missions, evangelism, Sunday school, youth programs, and worldwide service) to be biblical and vital. Our institutions of education, publication, hospitals, and homes are part of our commitment to the proclamation of the good news.

Applying the principles. How then can these basic elements of Amish retirement be translated into other options for those who do not live close to the soil? How can we have caring and sharing communities with the family scattered, urbanized, and "apartmentized"? Could the family be extended by co-opting "grandparents" or other persons into the nuclear family or spiritual and social fellowship? Could we in a world of gadgets be more selective and follow a more simple lifestyle? Simplicity should still be one of our most important teachings as a church, but it should cover our whole lifestyle and not just a few traditional concerns.

Selectivity might include simpler "death styles," as well as lifestyles. Could we become less dependent upon government—local, state, and national—and more dependent upon each other—old, young, and middle-aged—in caring and sharing? Could we come closer to nature by explaining her ways through small garden plots or raising small animals so that children actually see life at less than arm's length?

Could we share in more church and community projects for all ages which give spin-off effects similar to barn raisings or threshing bees? Many groups and congregations today are creative in this way. Mennonite Disaster Service and various projects of the Mennonite service and mission agencies have been innovative in including opportunities for older persons to continue their usefulness and develop a sense of continued integrity and fulfillment. Can we find alternatives to the "grandfather" house by intentional communities in which the elderly, middle-aged, and young live in close proximity, with special care for aging persons to help them live better independently? This is being done in a few instances but it takes planning and concern.

Restructuring the edifice complex

Health care programs and building complexes are not necessarily synonymous. There are "schools without walls," "churches without walls," even "prisons without walls," and there are some good models of "nursing homes and hospitals without walls." It takes more ingenuity on the part of boards, administrators, and staff to create and implement programs without walls than to construct an edifice which then may shape and too often determine programs. It's easy to think that every new program needs a new building.

We need to make better use of what we have before we build more, and to devise programs which do not need an edifice. In addition, the "baby boom" after World War II, which will greatly increase nursing care potential, should also affect our planning. From 1947 to 1957, 42,000,000 children were born in United States, 20 percent of our total population. Seventy-four percent of those children, over 31,000,000 persons, will reach the age of 65 from 2012 to 2022. By the year 2000 our population of persons sixty-five and above will increase 50 percent and by 2030 will more than double. With present policies governing admission to nursing homes, we would need 7,500 more such facilities by year 2000 and 15,000 more by year 2030. These are not wild guesses: these potential elders are now twenty-five to thirty-five years of age and in better health than ever before.

Alternatives are feasible

Some nursing homes and hospitals are now serving persons outside their walls. Institutions now established and certainly those in the planning stage should recognize that they are not free-standing institutions unrelated to other programs in the community. They can become mediums for the development of comprehensive services to the community and help meet the needs of nonresidents.

Service can be provided to a larger group of aged persons by developing day care programs in longtime care centers, hospitals, and other community agencies. Staff expertise combined with institutional resources can expand without enlarging facilities. Offering different levels of care promotes continuity of services and a smooth transition for the elderly person being served.
—Theodore H. Koff in *The Gerontologist*(February, 1974)

The religiously sponsored home for the aged could utilize its professional know-how, its facilities and its strength of tradition to expand its service to include the elderly living outside the institution.
—Howard B. Bram, *ibid.*

General philosophy

1. Far too large a share of the health care dollar is spent on institutionalization because alternatives are too limited or nonexistent.

2. The goal of service should be to help older citizens live better and longer independently.

3. We pay too little to help older persons live adequately at home, but frequently are willing to spend much more to send them to nursing homes, or other institutions, which cost much more. Whenever studies have been made, it has been found that many who are institutionalized would not need expensive nursing home services if there were alternatives, but there is no place else to go.

4. Personal care organizations have been successfully organized in many places which enable the elderly and others to receive some care in their own homes and to live there more adequately.

5. A public policy which rewards community living rather than institutional living by supplementing personal care resources has been successful in Western Europe, England, and the United States.

Home care services

The following home care services may be required if some retirees are to be able to continue living independently:

1. **Assistance in food shopping, meal preparation, menu planning, or home delivery of meals.**
2. **Mobility outside the home—transportation for activities, church, shopping, doctors, drugs. (The lack of transportation is one of older persons' largest problems.)**
3. **Laundry and home maintenance.**
4. **Home visits by doctors, visiting nurses, or home health aides under the direction of nurses or doctors.**
5. **Adult day-care centers.**
6. **Senior centers.**
7. **Nutrition programs.**
8. **Help in dressing and personal care.**
9. **Guidance in financial, legal, and housing matters.**
10. **Spiritual guidance and counsel including facing death realistically and with dignity.**
11. **Knowledge of available health and social services— including such assistance as food stamps.**
12. **Availability of help in times of crisis.**
13. **Assurance in many areas of fear and loneliness.**
14. **Suitable activities in recreation, education, and good use of leisure.**

Implementation

1. Churches, institutions, and community organizations could help study and plan the services needed and how they might be delivered.

2. Those who are retired could be used to help carry out some of these services on a part-time basis and add to their income. Certainly, the aged should help in the planning.

3. Unskilled persons could be used in giving help in a number of areas—home maintenance, maid service, cleaning and cooking, purchasing foods, general "chore" services.

4. Professional nurses, home economists, and social workers could supervise helpers and deliver services to significant numbers of older persons who need their services. Doctors could set up clinics at suitable locations a few hours a week to deal with a number of persons. Paraprofessionals could deliver many services under the direction of professionals.

5. Many women and men who are active and responsible could serve as live-in companions. An information bureau could be established to bring needs and resources together. Such an arrangement could provide good living conditions for the helpers as well as for the person requiring the services.

6. In a number of places large residences are being converted to efficiency apartments where three or four persons can live under one roof with privacy as well as companionship and help in time of need.

Home services are also costly

Home service programs have "a price tag" for the individual, the church, the community, and government. There is no such thing as a "free ride." However, if the time when one may have to enter a hospital or a nursing home can be postponed or prevented with some less costly alternate, expenses will be less and generally the patient will be served more effectively. In Great Britain geriatric day-care centers make up one part of an intricate network of elderly services that have successfully reduced the British nursing home population to 2 percent of those over sixty-five years of age.

Good nursing homes are important

Nursing homes are an important part of our health delivery service. Although less than 5 percent of those over sixty-five live in a nursing home at a given time, 20 percent will die in such an institution. (Nearly 50 percent of older persons die in hospitals; the rest die at home, on the road, or in miscellaneous places.) Generally, the need for institutional care comes late in life and advanced age is accompanied by physical frailty or mental illness or both. In 1977 the average age for nursing home entry was eighty-four.

Nursing homes, in spite of bright colors, modern equipment, and beautiful trappings, carry foreboding connotations to many patients. They are seen as "the end of the road." Even if a nursing home is the only choice left, persons hesitate to enter one. For older persons the thought of a nursing home brings youthful visions of the county home or the poor farm which most counties in the United States at one time provided as a shelter for the indigent who had no caring relatives or whose family deserted them. Since that time needs have changed, numbers have increased, families have changed, financing has changed, societal values—including those of the family and the church—have changed. However, the biblical teaching that we are to help care for older family members in an enlightened way has not changed. The church as the extended family should feel more responsibility than ever before.

There are times when it may be wrong to keep persons out of nursing homes. There are mental conditions and physical impairments which need the expertise potentially available in such an institution. However, some persons who may need the services of a nursing home are not able to afford it. Many such persons are hidden away trying to fend for themselves against overwhelming odds.

Some clients misplaced

Thousands of persons now in nursing homes are misplaced. A United States Senate report said, "Studies of the characteristics and needs of the nursing home population in Massachusetts and elsewhere in the country indicate that 15 to 20 percent of such persons are absolutely misplaced in the institutional environment."

Another statement in the report is extremely pertinent: "In many ways public welfare is a twentieth-century poorhouse without walls. As a result large numbers of the disabled are forced into nursing homes or mental hospitals at a very high charge to the public treasury, simply because public programs could not give attention to alternative ways of meeting their needs outside of an institution."

Kinds of nursing homes

Of the 20,000-plus nursing homes in United States, 74

percent are proprietory or private and must make a financial profit to stay in business. Twenty percent are nonprofit, sponsored by religious, fraternal, or community agencies, and 6 percent are operated by the government, particularly for veterans. The facilities and the scope of services vary tremendously. Some homes are sophisticated complexes, modern in every way, and others are old rambling houses renovated for a new purpose. The services vary from compassionate, enlightened, and adequate professional personal care with good food, comfortable and clean surroundings, to a minimum of professional and other services, poor food, unsanitary conditions—barely able to pass state inspection, even if warned ahead of time!

The exterior facade of a nursing home does not express the kinds of personal services provided. Many proprietory homes are good and some nonprofit ones are bad. However, a nonprofit home, particularly one operated by a religious body, has a distinct advantage in rendering services. A 1979 U.S. Census Bureau report said over 90 percent of the people in nursing homes are satisfied with their care and their surroundings. Living in a nursing home can be rewarding—if it's the right place, at the right time, with continuing family and community interest and support.

Levels of service

Nursing homes generally give two levels of care:

Skilled care: one step away from acute hospital care. Its clients are the most frail and most vulnerable of the nation's elderly. Round-the-clock nursing care is provided.

Intermediate care: these clients also are too frail or too ill to live at home without support services which a church, family, or community might provide. They need less professional nursing care and less staff time, but they may need routine help in getting in and out of bed, in bathing, dressing, walking, taking medications, and the like.

Some retirement centers include many types of apartments for independent living, or even semi-independent living, but these residents are not to be included as a part of the nursing home population. This kind of independent living, in fact, helps keep persons out of nursing homes.

INVOLVEMENT: Some operating models of housing options

There is almost no limit to housing options for older persons. The following examples might be helpful for older persons to look at in their future planning. Most older persons will likely find it necessary to use more than one option.

1. *Own home.* Approximately 75 percent of those over 65 or retired persons own their own homes and many continue to live independently throughout their days.

2. *Retirement centers.* Individuals live completely independent in a retirement center, often with more independence than in their own homes because they do not have to take care of maintenance, snow removal, lawn mowing, and so on.

3. *Condominiums.* Five families in Goshen, Indiana, have built a condominium and they have organized a corporation which sets up the rules. The inside of the structure belongs to individuals and can be maintained and developed as the individual decides. The roof, the walls, and the grounds are common property and are dependent upon corporation decisions.

4. *Home sharing.* Three widows, instead of each living in a separate unit or house, have renovated a large house into three separate apartments. One room is set aside for the activities of all.

5. *Duplex.* A couple built a new house with a separate unit for the parents. After the parents both died, the apartment was rented out.

6. *Triplex.* Two married children built a ranch home with three apartments. One couple lived at either end and the parents occupied the central apartment. The building was constructed in such a way that the central apartment could be divided effectively after the parents both died.

7. *Extended household.* Parents and married daughter and husband bought a good-sized house together. There are separate quarters, but in general both use common facilities. Most meals are prepared jointly. The household frequently entertains guests.

8. *Grandfather house.* In Old Order Amish practice a separate house owned by the parents is built next to or some-

times as a part of the home of one of the children.

9. *Apartments.* An older couple built two apartments, one for a younger couple. The younger couple does the maintenance work, mows the lawn, and performs certain other services for the older couple. The younger couple is reimbursed by receiving a subsidy in rent.

10. *Common grounds.* Three widows built separate houses on the same tract of land, living side by side. The backyard is common property and under common maintenance.

11. *Adult family care.* In the state of West Virginia individual family homes, selected by the Department of Welfare, are authorized and paid for by the state to provide a home for clients who have no responsible family ties, but who need a protective environment to bridge the gap between independent living and an institution.

12. *Apartment sharing.* A council on aging leases six three-room apartments to unrelated persons who cannot live alone for various reasons. None, however, needs round-the-clock nursing care; all manage with a part-time homemaker and a cleaning person.

STARTERS

1

About 30 percent of the older people in the U.S. live in substandard housing. These houses lack such items as running water, indoor toilets, and central heating. Some young people are giving one or more years as volunteers to rehabilitate older persons' homes on a pay-as-you-can basis. Some government programs are effective in a broad sense. Help has already started!

2

The 70 percent of older people in the U.S. who own their own homes rate property tax relief high on their list of housing needs. They also mention the mounting cost of energy to heat and maintain a home. What has your state done to provide relief? Whom have you thanked on behalf of the people for whom you go to bat—your parents, grandparents, and other older persons?

3

Group housing suited to the physical and economic needs of the frail old people who cannot live alone remains one of the least developed alternatives to institutional care. What is the community, church, or governmental body to which you belong doing to meet the need? Live-in assistance could be expanded with adequate funding.

4

Existing nursing homes are in an excellent position to seek ways of meeting social, psychological, and spiritual needs of older persons in ways that reach beyond the institution. What non-domiciliary services exist in your community? Ask your newspaper editor if none are apparent.

5

Some of the most traumatic family times come in the emotional decision to place a father or mother (or other member) in a nursing home—even after a rewarding life in various other living arrangements. About 20 percent of persons over sixty-five will use a nursing home, less than 5 percent at any one time. What help does the administration of the nursing home or your church or community agency give to make this transition? Don't accept easy answers. Remain part of the solution. After the fact, don't forget to visit family members and friends who have moved to the nursing center. Visitors, including children, are not only welcome, but they become a vital part of the care. Awareness of the human touch lasts a lifetime, even if some persons may not show overt signs of recognition. Some nursing homes have found that pets help foster a stimulating environment.

6

How would you apply the practices of the Amish to your interests and situation when retirement years come?

7

Seek ways to support the services of existing agencies or councils that deal with older people. These are key organizations in your community. Offer your help.

10 A Challenge to the Church

None need travel the journey of life alone. The relationships nurtured through healthy social interaction, within and beyond the family, hold the key to growing older with confidence, anticipation, and security. The choices are ours to make. We must accept responsibility for ourselves, balanced with appropriate concern for others.

The contemporary forces of depersonalization, individualism, loss, change, and mobility call all the more for promoting relationships that equally protect independence and provide for dependence. In belonging, we can be most ourselves, freed to give and to receive.

Life purpose

Each of us needs a purpose for living. The Christian can say with Paul, "For me to live is Christ, and to die is gain" (Philippians 1:21). Lack of meaning has been and continues to be the major affliction facing people of all ages. If uncorrected, the condition worsens with advancing years.

On the other hand, a lifetime of purposeful living can be enhanced in the later years. The best is yet to be. That's the challenge that falls to us, no matter what our age or circumstances. The best can yet be, given a purpose for living.

The simple truth

The late Karl Barth, world-renowned Swiss theologian, was

asked, "What is the greatest spiritual truth that came to you from lifetime study of theology?"

He answered, "Jesus loves me this I know for the Bible tells me so."

Christian basis for caring

For the Christian, responding first in faith then in discipleship to Christ's act of obedience, his death on the cross, brings freedom from guilt and purpose for living. In moving from unfaith to faith we enter into a covenant with God and with other Christians. In Christ we love one another, find our brothers and sisters, and serve them, inviting them to faith. Emulating Christ's love is the Christian's basis for caring. It is possible for two or three or even 300 or 3,000 who gather in Christ's name, to risk themselves and become covenant partners.

In no other body can unearned and unrepayable love accomplish the reasonable expectations of the church to feed the hungry, give drink to the thirsty, care for the forgotten and the helpless, clothe the naked, give shelter to those without houses, and heal the brokenhearted and the oppressed, whether friend or enemy. In humble acts of mercy and justice the mature Christian serves in the name of Christ without thought of personal benefit. If as members of the church we stoop to dishonest motives, we are unrighteous. There is no neutral ground. "He who is not with me is against me, and he who does not gather with me scatters" (Luke 11:23).

The church: A task for every age

The instructions in the book of Acts give to some, often the middle-aged, the task to prophesy—to preach, to give instruction in religious matters, to lead the way religiously and socially. This is not indicated as a task for men only. The apostle Paul said, "On the morrow we departed and came to Caesarea; and we entered the house of Philip the evangelist, who was one of the seven, and stayed with him. And he had four unmarried daughters, who prophesied" (Acts 21:8, 9).

Younger persons are not afraid to use the power of imagination and make suggestions. They are not restricted as some who have tried and failed and refuse to try again. The young can afford to take risks because the chances are good that they can fall without hurting themselves permanently, as would older persons with rigid fixations and brittle limitations.

The dreaming of dreams by older persons is not to be discounted. Dreams represent strongly desired goals and a better future. Older persons with tested wisdom can weigh possibilities, devise, confront, and project ways by which dreams may become realities.

Elders, a growing part of the church family

Older persons (sixty-five plus), the saints here and now, make up 15 to 25 percent of the average congregational membership. This percentage will increase by 50 percent in the next three decades. These persons have important linkages with the past, but are important segments of the church today. The "Fountain of Youth" is not in the realm of the physical or the biological, but in the kingdom of the intellectual, social, and spiritual.

Church leaders are increasingly recognizing the many resources, as well as some of the needs of aging persons. Older persons are real persons with real names, real resources, real needs—and they want to be thus identified. The single greatest need is to be involved and to be accepted and to feel useful in church and community. We do not terminate membership in the nuclear family or the congregational family as long as we have physical life and breath.

Five universal desires of the aging

In the late thirties Leo Simmons carried on significant research on aging from cross-cultural files at Yale University.

Simmons studied seventy-one preliterate cultures and concluded that there were five universal desires held by these cultures for older people: (1) to prolong life; (2) through the conservation of energy to find some rest and release from one's occupation; (3) to remain socially active; (4) to maintain control over one's property, one's authority, and one's prestige in the society; (5) eventually to seek an honorable death with reasonable expectation of a new and better existence in the hereafter.

Since the studies by Simmons the pace has quickened in all kinds of gerontological research. The universal desires which he found for the aging of the seventy-one preliterate cultures have been more carefully documented and may have become more sophisticated but they remain essentially appropriate today.

What the elders have gained

The Old Testament philosopher, in trying to answer the question of why the godly suffer, said, "In his hand is the life of every living thing and the breath of all mankind. Does not the ear try words as the palate tastes food? Wisdom is with the aged, and understanding in length of days" (Job 12:10-12). This does not imply that every person who is full of years is full of wisdom. Some older persons (and too many younger ones) have ceased to grow since their earlier years. However, we are never too old to grow unless disease (physical or mental) should cut us down, or we deliberately fail to use and amplify our gifts.

Wisdom is with the aged and understanding in length of days not because of unusual mental powers or endowments but because the elders have capacities that only years can bring:

1. *Perspective.* They have experienced a full lifetime, not a few thin slices of life.

2. *Objectivity.* There are no hidden agendas to serve as a front for seeking job promotions, higher wages, social rank, or to thwart competition.

3. *Experience.* The elders can sort out those things which have failed and those which have proven to be worthwhile and discard the excess.

4. *Tolerance and flexibility.* No group in recorded history has ever had to adjust to so many changes within a lifetime. Adapting to change means tolerance to other viewpoints and methods.

5. *To live better with less.* The great economic depression (1930-1940) tried the spirits and brought out the best and the worst. Those who could not adapt to severe conditions were wiped out, and even those who did survive economically and socially have been forever imprinted and influenced by the experience.

6. *Witness.* The elders have seen God's providence tested and proven.

7. *Forgiveness.* They have learned how to forgive and to be forgiven.

8. *To evaluate death.* They are closer to death and can accept this reality of life.

What can the church do about the elders?

1. Name them one by one and get a specific body of information about each. We can't help people in general. Ask your responsible denominational agency for assistance with materials or ideas.

2. What is your church now doing for or with older adults? What services are available in the church and in the community?

3. What are the obstacles? How can you help remove them?

4. What is the unique work of the church? If this gets done it has to be done now or it will be too late for some persons.

5. What should congregations do by themselves and what ought to be done with neighboring congregations?

6. What is your next step? Where are you going to dig in?

Voluntary simplicity

Most older persons were badly frightened by the depression of 1930 to 1940. They have never been able to put the depression out of their minds and have put too much dependence upon material things. Elders are carrying too much baggage along. Many younger people have learned they can "shed" more things and yet have much more than most of the people in this world. In this way things can become manageable and persons can become more free. Voluntary simplicity can be our goal and frugality and self-reliance will then prove that we can live better with less. Of course, we have to be careful in our priorities regarding the things that we shed. It is easy to replace some valuable things with those which are more convenient to carry.

Perspective

Ezekiel, the Old Testament prophet, went to Telabib. He reported, "I sat there overwhelmed among them seven days" (Ezekiel 3:15). At the end of the seven days he received his instructions from the Lord. Older persons have a perspective which younger persons will get only through the years. They have not been through the experiences that older persons have known.

Elders have seen most of the things which younger people have seen, although they haven't seen them through the same eyes. This doesn't mean that the vision of either older persons or younger persons is warped. It simply means that elders have sat where younger persons sit and thereby have gained a broad perspective which can be instructive to the whole congregation on rich and rewarding living.

Denominational effort

To identify denominational direction and priorities in relating with older persons a Mennonite Church Task Force on Aging (1977) made these recommendations:

---

1. **That there be an intensive program of calling the church to awareness of the special needs and resources of an aged population, living in retirement at a time of isolation and decreased activity.**

2. **That this program be directed to the entire brotherhood—pastors, church boards, agencies, high schools, colleges, and seminaries—coordinated by appropriate educational agencies and media.**

3. **That the educational process focus on whole-person needs and potentials, include goal-directed education for youth toward fullness of life, and utilize the life of our brotherhood to counter the fragmentation of society and the family.**

4. **That since the primary responsibility rests with congregations, each congregation be encouraged to form a council on aging to study its own problems, be informed about issues and resources, sponsor family life education on preparation for retirement, and investigate local solutions and options. Such a council should be part of or function in conjunction with a family life task group in the congregation.**

5. **That the denominational boards be encouraged to recruit and train persons to serve as counselors and instructors on aging to the brotherhood and its institutions. In light of unmet needs a full-time Mennonite gerontologist should be considered for appointment to a teaching**

(college), adviser (church), and consultant (agency) role.

**6. That before a community builds a domiciliary insti-
tution it consider alternative models that permit the aged
to live in a more free and satisfying manner, meeting
needs the individuals cannot supply alone without at the
same time taking from them the opportunities on which
their self-respect depends.**

**7. That specific help needs to be given to individuals,
families, and congregations in identifying, describing,
evaluating, and developing alternate models of living for
all of us, including senior citizens, if we are to retain or
regain a sense of spiritual community and wholeness of
life.**

**8. That existing institutions, such as nursing homes,
seek ways of meeting social, psychological, and spiritual
needs in addition to providing for material needs; that they
also seek ways of reaching beyond the institution to helping the needy of the community in nondomiciliary ways.**

INVOLVEMENT: The Warden Woods two-way street

The Warden Woods Church and Community Centre is on a
two-way street, solidly planted at one end of Fir Valley Court,
Scarborough, Ontario. For some people it is on the giving end of
the street. For others it is on the receiving end. And for those
most closely involved it is at one moment giving, at the next
receiving, and often both at once.

Richard Salzmann contributes varied skills. A concert
master during his life in Europe, at Warden Woods he has de-
lighted the Wednesday senior citizen club with his violin playing
ever since 1970. Major events like the annual Festival of Arts and
Crafts have been enhanced by his music. He has also taught
children the game of chess, throwing in a little German conversation.

After several years of such participation he found his way
into the Warden Park Church family, and his latter years are being enriched by the warmth of fellowship and the security of
many helping friends near at hand. At eighty-four he still plays
offertories at Sunday services.

Mrs. Smith found the Centre at the giving end of the street
when the public health nurse sent her over for social involvement. Now Maggie, who has cooked for a living since the age of

sixteen, comes twice a week to cook thirty dinners in the Centre kitchen for meals-on-wheels. She gets spiritual fulfillment in the act of providing meals for others, and she does it as a volunteer, for love.

It is a story of endless giving and receiving. The street to the Warden Woods Church and Community Centre is well used.

STARTERS

These practical suggestions will help develop a congregational action plan to meet the challenge of fulfilling membership for older persons and the entire congregation. The congregation should:

1

Seek to understand what has happened and is happening in the aging process. Developing proper attitudes toward aging and older persons starts with the young, but it also includes the attitudes of older persons toward themselves.

2

Play a more vigorous role in meeting the social and religious needs of older people. Some researchers have found that the typical sermon is geared to a family with children in the home. To feed the flock calls for consideration of all ages. Many older persons are widows, or otherwise singles. Quite often these persons, not deliberately, are treated in a demeaning manner. Most of the planning for social interaction is based on a couple concept. Some persons are shut-ins, which sometimes means to be shut out. Alert congregations can provide many spiritual and social highlights for these persons who may be the most needy and neglected.

3

Work out an educational program whereby the middle-aged, beginning at about age thirty, may be en-couraged to make plans for the retirement or disengagement years.

4

Take leadership in offering short-term courses for retired persons.

5

Give recognition to the fact that older persons are an independent breed with broad experience, who have adapted to more changes than occurred in the whole previous span of history, who do not want to ask for favors, but they do want a distinct voice in the planning which is done for them.

6

Officially designate and commission certain persons to study the resources and needs of the aging, and to act in their behalf. This should be an ongoing commission. It should include from five to seven persons, represent all adult age-groups, male and female, with staggered terms of office. This commission should establish a library on gerontology. There are magazines and books which church libraries should have.

7

Make a thorough individual survey to find the resources and the trouble spots of the aging. It is to be assumed that many aging and retired persons do not have special needs beyond those of other members, but all have resources which they would like to contribute. We don't know until we get the facts—let's get them!

8

Designate a certain day or days such as "Heritage Days" in which congregations give special attention to past contributions, to the present resources and needs of the aging, and to the gifts within the total congregation for ministering to aging persons.

9

Find a way to study together the theological and ethical aspects of responsibility for all persons in the congregation who have special needs. The aging would be embarrassed to have attention focused entirely upon their needs if it meant the neglect of other basic needs. This study might be called the "Theology of Caring."

10

Join with other congregations in pooling information regarding programs which might be better done cooperatively.

11

Make every effort to see that the church and Sunday school facilities take the needs of the aging and the handicapped into account. In new buildings and in renovations such factors as accessibility, mobility, safety, comfort, hearing aids, and sight-saving reading materials should be carefully planned. Transportation may be one of the physical barriers. The needs of the homebound must be planned for, also.

12

Give high priority to the outstanding resources of women in planning and implementation. Frequently women are more sensitive to needs, more resourceful, make better adaptations to retirement, read more widely, make friends easier, and better recognize nutritional and domestic needs; and nearly three fifths of the aged are women.

13

Provide opportunities for intergenerational contacts. The aging do not want to be sealed off from other generations.

14

Utilize the facilities and the resources available within the community to accomplish many things. The major creative resource is the willingness of persons to give a bit of themselves. We are quick to respond to the tragedies of nature: floods, droughts, earthquakes, and fires. The slow tragedies of human nature are not so dramatic but just as real. We hear much of balanced rations for livestock, conservation, and efforts to correct material pollution. Nutritional deficiencies, social erosion, and the pollution of the human spirit should bring a new sense of quickening to each of us.

# Dying and Death

In much literature dealing with this topic, the word sequence is death and dying. The sequence in the chapter title above is deliberate. Dying is a process, and death is a final physical action—a permanent cessation of all vital functions.

Death is a part of life. I am a dying person; so are you. Our physical lives are always terminal. There are significant differences in the years of our days on earth but the exact number is always somewhat irrelevant. "It is appointed unto men once to die, but after this the judgment" (Hebrews 9:27). "For as in Adam all die, so also in Christ shall all be made alive" (1 Corinthians 15:22). Our days on earth always have meaning, be they many or few. Our coming and our going are not without influence. "None of us lives to himself, and none of us dies to himself" (Romans 14:7).

Avoid isolation at death

Today half of our citizens die in hospitals, 20 percent in nursing homes, and 30 percent at home, on the road, on the job, or on trips. This completely reverses the pattern for dying of a generation or two ago. Through the past sixty years we have gone to great lengths to isolate persons from their loved ones at the time of death, the time they most need familiar surroundings, relatives, and friends. Eighty percent of deaths today are persons over sixty-five, and it may be easier to push older persons aside in the time of death than younger persons.

However, some more enlightened practices are beginning to emerge. David Guttman, psychologist at Northwestern University, said, "Americans have lately learned to humanize the poor, minorities, and others. Now we are realizing that the dying are the most dehumanized group of all."

In little more than a decade, the subject of death has moved out of the shadow of cultural taboo and onto the agendas of medical professionals, educators, the clergy and public policymakers. The movement's major achievement has been to make death a fit subject for public discussion. The dying themselves have become tutors to their own doctors and nurses, thanks largely to the pioneering work of Swiss-born psychiatrist Elizabeth Kübler-Ross, who has encouraged thousands of terminally ill patients to speak up about their needs and fears. The experience of dying is routinely explored in schools and dramatized in the media, threatening, as some say, "to turn the mystery of death into just another fad." And even government officials are now grappling with ways to end what California Governor Jerry Brown calls America's "apartheid system of isolating the terminally ill."
—Psychologist Robert Kastembaum in *Newsweek* (May 1, 1978), copyright 1978 by Newsweek, Inc. All rights reserved. Reprinted by permission

---

Stages of dying

Psychiatrist Elizabeth Kübler-Ross was one of the first definitive writers on dying and death. Her book, *On Death and Dying* (1969), was a best seller and the thanatology boom which followed made her famous worldwide. Her outline of the five stages of death have been accepted by college and hospital groups and many others who have made studies of this area. *The Ladies' Home Journal* chose Kübler-Ross as one of "eleven women of the decade" for the 1970s.

People pass through clearly defined stages in reconciling themselves to death, according to Kübler-Ross:

1. *Denial—"No, not me."* This is a typical reaction when a patient learns that he or she is terminally ill. Denial, according to Kübler-Ross, is important and necessary. It helps cushion the impact of the patient's awareness that death is inevitable.

2. *Rage and anger—"Why me?"* The patient resents the fact that others will remain healthy and alive while he or she must die. God is a special target for anger, since he is regarded as imposing, arbitrarily, the death sentence. To those who are shocked at her claim that such anger is not only permissible but inevitable, she replies succinctly, "God can take it."

3. *Bargaining—"Yes me, but...."* Patients accept the fact of death but strike bargains for more time. Mostly they bargain with God, "even people who never talked with God before." They promise to be good or to do something in exchange for another week or month or year of life. "What they promise is totally irrelevant, because they don't keep their promises anyway."

4. *Depression—"Yes, me."* First, the person mourns past losses, things not done, wrongs committed. But then he or she enters a state of "preparatory grief," getting ready for the arrival of death. The patient grows quiet and doesn't want visitors. "When a dying patient doesn't want to see you anymore," Kübler-Ross observes, "this is a sign he has finished his unfinished business with you, and it is a blessing. He can now let go peacefully."

5. *Acceptance*—"My time is very close now and it's all right." Kübler-Ross describes this final stage as "not a happy stage, but neither is it unhappy. It's devoid of feelings, but it's not resignation. It's really a victory."

Knowledge of these stages can help families and medical personnel understand what the dying person is going through and can help them aid rather than hinder the patient in achieving the kind of death he or she wants.

"Some want to go out fighting," says Kübler-Ross, "and they should. We should not try to impose our will on them. If you listen to the patient, he will tell you how he wants to die."

A change

More recently some of Kübler-Ross's activities and conclusions have become suspect by her colleagues. *Time* magazine (November 12, 1979) said, "In recent years Kübler-Ross had a conviction that the living could communicate with the dead and she began to dabble in spiritualism at her retreat north of San

Diego. She now refers to herself as an 'immortal visionary and modern cartographer of the River Styx, and she has apparently lost any remaining credibility with her professional colleagues." If this change is true, it need not nullify the value of her previous concepts which were tested by many and accepted widely. The five "Stages of Dying" seem to be valid.

What is death like?

Jill Leichty, a twenty-five-year-old admissions counselor at Goshen College, died of leukemia in 1977. She was a beautiful, vivacious young woman, filled with the Holy Spirit, who had every reason to want to live. Before her death she wrote to the college newspaper, "I've learned a lot in the last three months and I thank God that He has been so near to me. I do not fear what lies beyond this life because I have a perfect peace about that. God has come to me and given me the gift of peace. I think it is your prayers that have allowed that to happen. That's a miracle."

Prepared to die and wanting to die, not synonymous

It is difficult to motivate middle-aged persons to take a square look at the question of facing the later years. Old age seems threatening and aging and death are closely associated in their minds. Persons who have made their peace with their Creator and their fellowmen are not afraid to die, but usually they do not want to die. There is a great deal of difference between being ready to die and wanting to die.

The desire to live is strong. One of the consultants for this article says that in twenty-five years of practice he cannot remember a single patient—elderly or not elderly—asking him to end his life or to take direct action to stop whatever is keeping him alive. Relatives have asked him to 'take Dad out of his pain,' but the patient himself has never made the request."
—Abigail Fowler in *Patient Care* (March 15, 1978)

In the final hours

Most older persons who are prepared to meet their Creator do not have unreasonable fears about death—they know death is part of life, life both here and hereafter. But they are anxious that in their last hours they are not abandoned, or allowed to pass away without dignity or even unnoticed. All persons have a deep sense of dignity and self-esteem which they fear may be violated in the time of death. Also they resent facing death in the impersonal atmosphere of a hospital or nursing home with loved ones thrust aside as medical workers feverishly attempt to squeeze out the last gasp of breath by heroic means and equipment. If persons in their final hours are conscious, they desperately need and want understanding loved ones to be near to communicate by their presence and by holding hands that they are passing on in dignity and are not abandoned.

The hospice movement

In the middle ages religious orders established hospices to care for travelers, as well as for ailing and dying pilgrims. The hospice offered an open door to the sick, the dying, the hungry, the wayfarer, the needy poor.

The first modern hospice was London's St. Christopher's Hospice founded by Dr. Cicely Saunders in the early nineteen sixties. Modern hospices have the objective to help people die with as little discomfort and as much "at homeness" as possible. The first hospice in the United States was established in 1971 in New Haven, Connecticut; however, it operated without a building of its own until 1979.

Two thirds of the patients of Hospice, Inc., die at home, surrounded by their families and free of technological life-prolonging devices. Hospice provides service twenty-four hours a day, seven days a week. The availability of emergency medical, nursing, and various counseling services gives patients the security and support they need to continue home care.

    —Sylvia Ann Lack, Medical Director Hospice, Inc., New Haven, Connecticut

---

Hearing the dying

If the living are to be most helpful to those who are dying, we should have some understanding of death. We should learn how to listen, what to listen for, how to be supportive without too many words, how to recognize and empathize in the various stages dying persons go through. Being really helpful requires compassion, deliberation, understanding, and common sense.

Lord, grant that I may seek rather to comfort than to be comforted; to understand than to be understood; to love than to be loved; for it is by giving that one receives; it is by forgetting that one finds; it is by forgiving that one is forgiven; it is by dying that one awakens to eternal life.
—St. Francis of Assisi

Carolyn Jo Dorr, a sociologist at Boston University, said she worries about people who say, "Throw me out to sea when I die." Dorr observes that such persons scorn ritual but leave no path for their survivors to follow.

The concern for survivors and how they overcome grief has become a major issue in North America. Some want to get away from the conventional funeral because they feel it subjects family and friends alike to ritualized morbidity.

In one study of 563 widows and widowers, thanatologist Robert Fulton found that those who opted for conventional funerals, with the body exposed for mourning, had fewer post-mortem adjustment problems and a more positive memory of the deceased than those who chose a closed casket or immediate disposition. Although few thanatologists insist that everyone ought to select funerals in which the casket is open, most scholars believe that the traditional practices of acknowledging death through ritualized mourning, as in Irish wakes and Jewish shivas, are more therapeutic and life-enhancing than quick burial.

The major drawback to most American funerals, says Dr. Herman Feifel, a clinical psychologist at the University of Southern California and the dean of U.S. thanatologists, is that the period of ritualized mourning does not last long enough. "My studies show that grief lasts a minimum of about two years, yet our funeral rites last only a week or a month at most," he says.

Death gives meaning to life

From *Christopher News Notes* comes the following account: Elena Frings, a young woman in her twenties, was informed by her doctor that her heart was so weak that she had only six months to live. She decided to leave her office job in Santiago, Chile, and work as a volunteer community organizer among the city's slum dwellers.

"That way I will die happy," she told a friend.

Frings worked so effectively that she was invited to New York to give talks about the program. There she met a surgeon who successfully operated on her defective heart.

Elena Frings is now back in South America, helping the poor who live on the margins of society. It was her expectation of death—not the operation—that gave new meaning and direction to her life.

President Roosevelt left detailed instructions for his funeral and burial, should he die while president. He directed that the funeral service be simple, that the casket be plain and of wood, that there be no embalming of the body or sealing of the casket, and that his grave have no lining.

These instructions were found in a private safe days after his burial, too late to be considered. Consequently, Franklin D. Roosevelt's remains were embalmed, sealed in a copper coffin and placed in a cement vault.

—From *The Price of Death,* Consumer Survey Handbook 3, 1975, U.S. Superintendent of Documents

---

Special instructions

Not only is it important to make plans for our imminent death, but it is equally important for those left behind to know about these plans and where they are accessible. President Franklin D. Roosevelt made careful plans for his funeral which, unfortunately, were not carried out.

How to preplan a funeral

While death is inevitable, extremely high funeral costs need not be. Most funeral directors we meet, particularly in our smaller communities, are our neighbors and friends and are making a living legitimately. These persons will answer questions we should be asking before an emergency arises. The Purdue

University Extension Department of Consumer Affairs gives the following suggestions:

How do you go about preplanning a funeral? First, you should decide what type of service would be most fitting. The traditional service with an open or closed casket? A memorial service without the presence of a body? Or some form of service in between?

When you have an idea of the type of service you want, talk to a reputable local mortician. Discuss the type of service you have in mind, and ask him what the total cost would be.

The mortician will probably offer to take you on a tour of his facilities. Such a tour will give you a good idea of what he has to offer.

Most funeral directors will first take you to a casket show-room where you can see the available styles—and their prices. The cost of the casket alone can range from $200 to many thousands. Look carefully; the cost of the casket is the basic funeral expenditure.

Ask the funeral director what the casket price includes. It may include the total price of the standard or regular adult funeral service. The following services may or may not be included in the total price, so be sure to ask:

1. Removal of the body to the funeral home.
2. Burial permits and death certification.
3. Embalming.
4. Use of the funeral home facilities, including viewing room and chapel.
5. Clothing for the deceased.
6. Cosmetic work to restore the appearance of the body.
7. Transportation of the body to a cemetery within a certain distance.
8. The services of the funeral director.
9. Scheduling church services.
10. Receiving and displaying flowers.
11. Transportation of the flowers to the cemetery.
12. Use of the hearse.
13. An organist.
14. A limousine for the family.
15. Grave or mausoleum crypts.

16. Notices to the radio and newspaper.
17. Vault.
18. Grave marker.

Many of these services may be considered as "extra service." If so, make a note of the cost of each service. Before you complete any transaction, get an itemized list of the services and the cost of each. Be sure you know the *total cost,* including interest and finance charges if applicable.

Obviously, this entire endeavor would be much easier if not conducted under shaken, grief-stricken circumstances. However, if you are caught without any funeral plans at the time of need, take a close friend—preferably an experienced businessman or lawyer—with you to make plans. Or have him represent you.

Check burial benefits

As you consider funeral costs, remember that you may be eligible for burial benefits from the federal government. Federal agencies provide burial benefits to about half the people who die each year. To find out if you are eligible, check with your local health officer.

Some will not be objective

Even written instructions, written with suggestions from those who may not have been completely unbiased, can be bent beyond the obvious intent and interest of the deceased. An Illinois bachelor farmer died some years ago leaving an estate of approximately eight million dollars. His will carried a statement to the effect that his funeral should be somewhat in keeping with and commensurate to other funerals of those of comparable economic status. The funeral cost more than $30,000—about the same as Elvis Presley's. A court suit followed, but it was difficult to prove that those who carried out the will went beyond the letter of the instructions and the suit was dropped. However, nearly everyone in the community believed that someone within the ranks profited personally. The deceased, so frugal in his lifetime that on occasion he used binder twine for shoelaces, would never have believed that such a situation could arise.

In another case the deceased left a will with instructions that an educational institution was to share his estate along with nieces and nephews. One of the nephews involved helped set up the will for his uncle and had it so arranged that all expenses for processing would be taken from the cash residue rather than the 160 acres each niece and nephew was to receive. Unfortunately, the educational institution didn't receive a very large grant.

The living will

In most cases loved ones want to do everything possible to help sustain the life of family members as long as possible, even in terminal illness. In certain situations we go to extraordinary means to sustain life when it is evident that the body is vegetating or that there is great pain with no earthly hope of relief. Family members are reluctant to suggest that extraordinary means should be discontinued, even though there is great suffering and death is imminent. However, a properly executed document made at a time of full understanding can be of great value to the family. This instrument is sometimes called a living will. It is not a will and has no legal status; however, it does carry ethical implications.

In no case is the living will a form of euthanasia. Euthanasia implies that something is done covertly to shorten a person's life. Neglecting to use extraordinary machines or asking that such machines be unplugged is quite a different matter. The living will is what the individual who composed it would like to have happen and often this suggestion saves the family a great deal of trauma. The living will included below may be used as a guide, with whatever personal changes one may wish to include.

TO MY FAMILY, MY PASTOR, MY DOCTOR, MY LAWYER
If the time comes that I am unable to take part in decisions for my own future and there is no reasonable expectation of recovery from terminal illness, let this statement stand as a testament of my wishes:
I request that I be allowed to die a natural death and not be kept alive by artificial means or heroic and extraordinary measures. Death is a reality of life as are birth, growth, maturity, old age, and it is ordained by God that man shall once physically die. I *do not* fear death. I do long to see my Creator and my Redeemer whenever my earthly journey becomes meaningless. *I do* abhor the indignity of

mental and physical vegetation with dependence on machines when recovery is beyond hope and the body continues to be racked with pain. The heavy expense of applying extraordinary measures in terminal illness to me represents poor stewardship and may place a heavy financial load upon my family with which I would not wish to burden them.

I also ask that pain-killing drugs should be mercifully administered to me in terminal suffering, even at the expense of a few hours of my life.

If my last days should be spent in a hospital or a nursing home, if it seems reasonable and not too much of a burden to my loved ones, I would like to spend my final hours in familiar surroundings with loved ones near me.

This request is made while I am in good health and spirits. Although this document is not legally binding, you who care for me will, I hope, feel morally bound to follow its mandates. I recognize that it places a heavy burden of responsibility upon you, and it is with the intention of sharing that responsibility and of mitigating any feelings of guilt that this statement is made.

Signed:
Date:
Witness:
Witness:

INVOLVEMENT: "In the house of the Lord forever . . ."

Frequently, a dying person is surrounded by medical personnel or even relatives but no one is communicating. Words at a time like this are not important, but tangible forms of presence and empathy do communicate to the dying person. This is the time when, regardless of one's financial or social standing, all are equal.

Jacob A. Schowalter, a bachelor, reputed to have been the first Mennonite millionaire, died in the Bethel Hospital, Newton, Kansas, in 1953. Schowalter left his entire estate (the Schowalter Foundation) to three church groups.

Elizabeth Spicher, now of Overland Park, Kansas, was the attendant nurse at his death. A student nurse was the only other person present in the hospital room. When Mrs. Spicher saw that Schowalter was dying, she took hold of his hand and started repeating the Twenty-third Psalm. After repeating "The Lord is my shepherd," she saw that Schowalter was passing rapidly and she moved to "surely goodness and mercy shall follow me all the days of my life; and I shall dwell in the house of the Lord forever." Mrs. Spicher felt a slight squeeze on her hand and Jacob Schowalter's spirit took flight.

STARTERS

1

"It is my eager expectation and hope . . . that with full courage now as always Christ will be honored in my body, whether by life or by death," the apostle Paul said (Philippians 1:20). Jill Liechty quoted that verse shortly before her death. Can it be your motto, too?

2

In the early history of North America, death nearly always took place in the home with all family members, including the children, entering into the experience. What ways has your congregation, denomination, or community developed for persons to accept and experience death as their familiar, ordinary, and expected destiny?

3

Sister Joyce Ann De Shano, a hospital chaplain in Detroit, Michigan, says that everyone experiences many deaths. She notes that after birth we pass the stage of complete dependence; at about five years old, we pass from the blanket and thumb to school; in adolescence, we give up childish ways; and as adults, we pass away from teenage thoughts and feelings. "Then we enter the state of 'aging,' " Sister Joyce observes, "and must give up some of our adult feelings." Then comes life-after-death. Sister Joyce suggests that one can help dying persons by not letting them die "without knowing you love them and care for them. Include them in the family decisions. Don't move in too fast. They don't want their decisions made for them. Sit down as close to their bed as you can when visiting with them. Don't be afraid to touch them and to share with them. Be sure to listen carefully to share where they are."

4

Discuss your fears and hopes for death with your family and small circle of friends. Do they know your wishes and feelings?

5

Some persons through certain religious beliefs and others through lack of belief find it necessary to deny death. Examine your own thoughts. What will it take for you to be ready to die?

6

If you have made arrangements for your funeral, you will have examined and considered the details of the funeral service itself, the grave space and cemetery costs, the grave marker. You will have become versed about embalming and cremation practices, the potential for organ and tissue donation, grave liners and vaults, and more. Are your plans accessible to those who will be responsible for your funeral?

12 Wisdom to Live By

Where do you want to be in twenty, or thirty, or forty years? If you plan earlier, old age is apt to come later. Some persons spend more time planning for a two-week vacation than they do for their later years. They don't plan to fail; they fail to plan.

The best preparation for fulfillment, joy, and peace in the retirement years is to live abundantly in every stage of life. We should experience meaningful living now, regardless of our birth date. We learn by doing and by experiencing at every moment in life.

Wisdom from Proverbs

In thinking through principles which I have found to be a vital part of the lifelong aging process, the Wisdom Literature of the Bible, particularly the book of Proverbs, came to mind. I read through Proverbs and selected verses to match with life-living principles of my own. Some matchings may be farfetched, yet in each case the essential point intended is to show that principles learned early in life determine the quality of life later. "A word fitly spoken is like apples of gold in a setting of silver" (Proverbs 25:11).

1. We are created in God's image. God did not create nobodies. "No one can ever make you feel inferior without your permission. Our own attitudes are the only thing about us that no one else can control," Eleanor Roosevelt said. "A man's pride

will bring him low, but he who is lowly in spirit will obtain honor" (29:23).

2. Realize in your early years that your way of living will determine what kind of an older person you will be. We take ourselves with us as we go on, baggage and all. "A man's mind plans his way, but the Lord directs his steps" (16:9).

3. Plan carefully for later years and retirement careers. This period may be a third of your life. "In everything a prudent man acts with knowledge, but a fool flaunts his folly" (13:16).

4. We are a part of all that we have touched and all that has touched us. Through faith and trust in God we are able to transcend, as well as make sense of, the temporal. "Every word of God proves true; he is a shield to those who take refuge in him" (30:5).

5. We need a healthy curiosity. We should cultivate broad interests. Narrow scholarship has its place, specialization its virtues, but literacy is significant in broad areas. Read widely, travel, serve, explore, listen, and study. It's hard to learn much from an easy book. "A wise man is mightier than a strong man, and a man of knowledge than he who has strength" (24:5).

There is no frigate like a book,
To take us lands away
Nor any coursers like a page
Of prancing poetry.
—Emily Dickerson, 1830-1885

---

6. Flexibility is an important law of life. Amenability to change does not imply a lack of principle. Compromise in method is the only way a democratic society can be maintained. "With patience a ruler may be persuaded, and a soft tongue will break a bone" (25:15).

7. Believe in yourself. Develop an appropriate self-image, not too high and not too low, not too tart and not too sweet. Seek a sober, well-balanced judgment. "A man's gift makes room for him and brings him before great men" (18:16).

8. Self-reliance and dependence are important. We should learn to do things for ourselves which are appropriate to do individually, but also we must recognize when it is best to involve

others. We must learn how to receive help graciously. "He who tends a fig tree will eat its fruit, and he who guards his master will be honored" (27:18).

9. Learn the art of forgiving others and yourself. We can ill afford to carry grudges. They transmit gloom to our souls and cause physical and mental disease. "A cheerful heart is a good medicine, but a downcast spirit dries up the bones" (17:22).

10. At times it pays to look back. What legacy have our forebears left? What lasting values have been passed on? To forget our history would be like losing our memory. "Remove not the ancient landmark which your fathers have set" (22:28).

11. Learn the rules of good mental and physical health early. We should learn how to deal with stress. "The fear of the Lord prolongs life, but the years of the wicked will be short" (10:27).

12. Our physical and mental health is personal, but it is not private. How we treat our bodies and minds has implications—social, spiritual, and economic—for the community and the church. Temperance and self-discipline are important. "If you have found honey, eat only enough for you, lest you be sated with it and vomit it" (25:16).

13. We must be able to lay aside some (not all) current satisfactions and pleasures in favor of reaching long-range goals or satisfactions. "Take heed to the path of your feet. . . . Do not swerve to the right or the left" (4:26, 27).

14. Financial planning is important early in life. Even a child should learn to do three things with an allowance—spend some, save some, give some. "A little sleep, a little slumber, a little folding of the hands to rest, and poverty will come upon you like a robber, and want like an armed man" (24:33, 34).

15. Learn to use leisure effectively in earlier years. The good use of leisure has to be learned and practiced before more free time is thrust upon us. "A tranquil mind gives life to the flesh, but passion makes the bones rot" (14:30).

16. Hard physical and mental activity, properly tempered with good judgment, is not apt to hurt us. "Discretion will watch over you; understanding will guard you" (2:11).

17. Learn to accept and deal with failure—your own and others'. Don't brood too long—just long enough to learn. "Pride

goes before destruction, and a haughty spirit before a fall" (16:18).

18. Continue to assess your talents honestly. Get your peers to help you be objective. "In an abundance of counselors there is safety" (11:14b).

19. Christian ethics are not accepted as universally as are scientific laws, yet application of the basic moral principles in the New and Old Testaments is as astounding and true as any scientific law. "If your enemy is hungry, give him bread to eat; and if he is thirsty, give him water to drink; for you will heap coals of fire on his head, and the Lord will reward you" (25:21, 22).

20. We must not make a rigid practice of comparing ourselves with others. We must be our own persons and make the best use of our own resources which are completely different from those of any other person. We must not shy away from unpleasant tasks in putting our gifts to work. "Drink water from your own cistern, flowing water from your own well" (5:15).

21. Learn how to live when you are by yourself. Aloneness and loneliness are not synonymous. "Let your foot be seldom in your neighbor's house, lest he become weary of you and hate you" (25:17).

22. We shouldn't be afraid to try something new because of a fear of failure. Risk-taking should not be equated with foolhardiness. "Hope deferred makes the heart sick, but a desire fulfilled is a tree of life" (13:12).

23. Learn to talk about the interests of others. If you concentrate only on yourself you will become boring. "He who guards his mouth preserves his life; he who opens wide his lips comes to ruin" (13:3).

24. Learn to accept success with humility, gratified but never completely satisfied. There is always room to improve. "If you have been foolish, exalting yourself, or if you have been devising evil, put your hand on your mouth" (30:32).

25. Learn the importance of small things, the little acts of kindness shown day to day. Learn how to express thanks and gratitude. Small can be beautiful! "A glad heart makes a cheerful countenance" (15:13).

26. Develop a sense of humor. Don't take yourself too seriously—take responsibilities seriously, but be able to laugh at

your own silly mistakes. At times we should admit unashamedly and unreluctantly that we were wrong. "Anxiety in a man's heart weighs him down, but a good word makes him glad" (12:25).

27. Our resources are given us as a trust. In serving the needs of others we serve ourselves. We need have no fear of becoming helpless, for even in being served we are worthy sons and daughters of God. "He who gives to the poor will not want" (28:27a).

28. Have close friends and make new friends regardless of race, color, creed, sex, and age. "A friend loves at all times, and a brother is born for adversity" (17:17).

29. Learn and practice the art of becoming a good listener. You will learn much and give the other person a sense of well-being. "If you are wise, you are wise for yourself" (9:12a).

30. Learn to guard your tongue if you want a few close friends at the end. "May my words be tender and well-seasoned, for tomorrow I may have to eat them," someone has said. "The mind of the righteous ponders how to answer" (15:28a).

31. There is a good deal of difference between being a healthy physical specimen and a whole person. Obviously, our goal should be to become whole persons. "The fear of the Lord is the beginning of knowledge; fools despise wisdom and instruction" (1:7).

32. Christian women and men should seek to make the other person—young or old, rich or poor, black or white, elite or of humble origin—feel comfortable in their presence. "The rich and the poor meet together; the Lord is the maker of them all" (22:2).

33. Seek opportunities and accept the responsibility to be involved in worthwhile things in your church and community. You are your brothers and sisters keeper. "A good name is to be chosen rather than great riches, and favor is better than silver or gold" (22:1).

34. We are always role models, particularly for our children and grandchildren. Generally a child's concept of God comes from parents. "Train up a child in the way he should go, and when he is old he will not depart from it" (22:6).

35. Nearly any reasonable expectation for an individual, a community, or a church can be accomplished if we use the right

methods, the right timing, achieve a consensus of the common sense of the common people, and if we don't care who gets the credit. "Let another praise you, and not your own mouth; a stranger, and not your own lips" (27:2).

36. Absorb as much international information and experience as possible. All persons everywhere create one world. "Righteousness exalts a nation, but sin is a reproach to any people" (14:34).

37. Don't try to judge people's motives. Keep your reservations to yourself. "A prudent man conceals his knowledge" (12:23a).

38. We shouldn't point out the failures of other persons to prop up our own egos. It is an easy habit to acquire and a tough one to shake. "Hatred stirs up strife, but love covers all offenses" (10:12).

39. Happiness is a by-product of serving others. Albert Schweitzer said, "I cannot predict your destiny, but I can predict that you will never be happy until you have served your fellowman." "Happy are those who keep my ways" (8:32b).

40. Pay the least possible attention to destructive remarks others may make about you. Live in such a way that no one will believe them. Forget about your "just dues." "Good sense makes a man slow to anger, and it is his glory to overlook an offense" (19:11).

41. Promises should be sacred and the way we carry them out establishes our character. Character is of supreme worth— not wealth, power, or position. "He who walks in integrity walks securely" (10:9a).

42. Life is a journey. We never arrive. Death is a part of living. "Do not boast about tomorrow, for you do not know what a day may bring forth" (27:1).

43. We are never too old or too young to grow in wisdom, stature, and favor with God. "The fear of the Lord leads to life; and he who has it rests satisfied" (19:23a).

44. Difficult as it may seem, we win by praying for those who hate us and by doing good to those who would harm us. This is part of the wisdom of a redeeming life measured in the realities of both time and eternity. "Do not rejoice when your enemy falls" (24:17a).

45. You have the last word in favor of growing older. Live it! "A word fitly spoken is like apples of gold in a setting of silver" (25:11).

INVOLVEMENT: The exemplary Samuel

Reread the story of Samuel in the Old Testament. You will recall the circumstances surrounding his birth and his early ministering in the temple under Eli. Who of us at the end of our days would not want to be counted worthy and vindicated by our people as was Samuel? Such a trust remains with us, to do honor to others and be reckoned worthy in our latter days.

And Samuel said to all Israel, "Behold, I have hearkened to your voice in all that you have said to me, and have made a king over you. And now, behold, the king walks before you; and I am old and gray, and behold, my sons are with you; and I have walked before you from my youth until this day. Here I am; testify against me before the Lord and before his anointed. Whose ox have I taken? Or whose ass have I taken? Or whom have I defrauded? Whom have I oppressed? Or from whose hand have I taken a bribe to blind my eyes with it? Testify against me and I will restore it to you." They said, "You have not defrauded us or oppressed us or taken anything from any man's hand." And he said to them, "The Lord is witness against you, and his anointed is witness this day, that you have not found anything in my hand." And they said, "He is witness."

—1 Samuel 12:1-5.

STARTERS

1

How effectively are you living? What ways have you found to respond to the challenge of adding positively to your years and helping others achieve the same?

2

In some dealings with people—your spouse, parents, or children perhaps—you've been less than wise. Wisdom comes from recognizing and correcting our mistakes and learning from them. Never avoid the risk of seeking reconciliation. Now is the time to act.

3

List how the material in this book is helping you plan for retirement years and how it has enabled you to better help older persons. Grade yourself A,

B, or C. What grade do you yet want to achieve?

4

How is your congregation responding to the challenge of the increasing number of elders in your midst? Support a ministry with such persons and expect hard work, some mistakes, and an infusion of new life in your congregational circle.

5

Are you tempted to draw back from the challenge of creative aging because someone else or some other group seems to have an edge on this? Start where you are. Anticipate the best God has in store for you—

mediated through the familiar and the new. Be open to the ways you can live fully by living for others. Take the first step.

6

Listen to the wisdom of those around you whom you might have thought of only as frail, old, young, foreign, a different color, learned, unlearned. As you see people in a new light, your life will take on a new character. It's largely a matter of the mind—attitude. Your mind can improve with age.

7

What kind of person do you want to be at ninety-one? You're on your way!

Appendices

HOW TO USE THIS BOOK FOR GROUP STUDY

To allow the insights of this book to become effective in family, congregational, and community life, group study of the issues included in this volume is recommended. In planning for such a study the leadership will need to help the group to develop their plans in the following areas.

1. Goals and objectives

In defining your goals and objectives for study, review the preface where the author lists the three foci of the book. In line with these, the goals and objectives for a class may include such areas as (a) development in self-understandings of the class members' situation in life and their roles as change agents in the congregation or community, (b) identification and development of action plans designed to encourage personal initiative and the use of personal resources in relation to the topic under discussion, and (c) shaping appropriate action plans for members, families, the congregation, and the community.

2. Formation of classes

Options for determining the composition of classes include:

a. *An elective class.* In an elective class, members interested in the topic form the study group. Leaders can assume a rather high degree of motivation and interest on the part of class members.

b. *An intergenerational class.* In such a group, representatives of two or more generations become involved. Such a group allows for the cross-fertilization of ideas of the young, middle-age, and older members. Leaders of this class will need to anticipate much diversity of experience, perspectives, and expectations. Action plans may be more personal or generational in nature. Several may need to be processed at the same time.

c. *A generational class.* In such a class members of similar ages become involved with one another. This provides a common base out of which to view the issues. Here cooperative group action plans are more possible.

d. *A congregational class.* A class composed of members of the same congregation or denomination allows their common theological and cultural understandings to mold their insights. It reflects the premise that the issue is spiritual in nature and is part of the ongoing life of the community of faith.

e. *A community class.* A class composed of members of the community allows for the cross-fertilization of ideas. It reflects the premise that the issue is broad and needs to be considered by all regardless of religious or cultural values and perspectives. Since assumptions and attitudes are diverse, progress toward agreement on the issues may be slow. But sharing and mutual growth in the understanding of the issues involved can make this approach worthwhile.

3. Class size

Size will vary according to the goals and objectives of the study. Smaller classes will allow for greater flexibility in planning, in the carrying out of action plans, and in sharing of personal experiences.

4. Time and place

Time and place of the study will depend upon the goals and objectives for it. Options include (a) a weekly meeting during the regular Sunday morning educational hour in the congregation, (b) a weekly evening meeting where an extended period of time is often available for consideration of the issue, (c) a weekend retreat using the facilities of the congregation or a retreat setting to provide a concentrated study of the issues, as well as an awareness for in-depth relationships of members of the study group; (d) a concentrated series of meetings in which the group meets nightly on consecutive nights for the duration of the study.

5. Leadership

Leadership selected for the study will need to be designated on the basis of the goals and objectives of the study and the type of class that is envisioned. A team reflecting various ages and a variety of experience and expertise in dealing with the issues will offer broader possibilities in fulfilling the intent of the study.

6. Resources

The text is the basic resource for study. All participants in the study need to have the contents of the text well in hand in order to benefit fully from it. Leaders should review the text carefully to discover the possible additional resources needed to conduct a satisfactory study experience. In the consideration of resource leaders, regard class members (their experiences and insights) as the basic human resource. Invite additional personnel from outside the class to contribute as needed. Include those who carry a special interest in the older person such as health, financial, governmental, and legal experts. Pastors, chaplains, and others routinely involved with older persons in the ministry of the church should also be invited to participate.

7. The study session

An outline for each study session may include:

a. Scripture readings and meditations related to the issue under consideration.

b. Establishment of session goals and objectives, with member commitment and participation to achieve them.

c. Review of the content of the chapter through methods (lecture, field trip, interview, and other) which are appropriate to leadership and members of the study group.

d. Review of the case study presented in "Involvement."

e. Consideration of action plans included in "Starters" with each member committing himself to carry out one of the suggested ideas (or one which he has developed) before the group meets again. Make clear that their participation in these action plans is to be reported at the next meeting. (What did they do? How did the older person feel? How did they feel? What was the impact? What did they learn about the older person and themselves?)

f. Consideration of the implications of the study for what is being done or should be done to enrich the situation of older persons in the life of the congregation and in the community. (The final study session should include the formulation of recommendations for further consideration or implementation by the congregation or agency of the community.)

—James E. Horsch, editor,
Congregational Literature Division,
Mennonite Publishing House

Appendix 2

DEMOGRAPHIC INFORMATION AND INTERPRETATION

U.S. Population 65 and Above*
July 1981

Year	Total Population	Life Expectancy	Median Age**	%65 and Above	Population 65 and Above
1800	5,300,000	35 yrs.	16.0	1.1	58,000
1850	23,190,000	40 yrs.	18.9	2.5	575,000
1900	76,000,000	47.3 yrs.	23.4	4.1	3,115,000
1950	151,000,000	68.2 yrs.	30.2	8.1	12,230,000
1980	226,500,000	74.0 yrs.	31.0	11.0	25,000,000
2000	260,378,000	75.0 yrs.	35.0	12.2	31,822,000***
2030	300,349,000	75.0 yrs.	40.0	17.0	51,000,000***

*   Canada's population is slightly more youthful than that of U.S. Accordingly, their data percentages are slightly lower. Ten-plus percent are over 65.
**   Half above, half below.
***   This data is from the medium protection service. Source: U.S. Census Bureau. Current population Reports, Series P-25, No. 704, July 1977, p. 70.

Growth in numbers
From 1900 to 1980 the total U.S. population increased nearly three times (76,000,000 to 226,500,000), and the sixty-five and over population increased 7.9 times (3,175,000 to 25,000,000).

Daily there are more than 5,000 arrivals at sixty-five and 3,700 departures from the sixty-five and above age category, a net annual increase of half a million.

Reasons for Percentage Increase of older persons
1. Better health care and better health.
2. Minimum loss of children in infancy and mothers in birth. In 1979 only 290 U.S. mothers died from childbirth or from complications of pregnancy. Only 45,000 infants out of 3,473,000 live births died in their first year.[1]
3. We have virtually eliminated most childhood and many adult diseases. In 1775 about 50 percent of the children died before reaching the age of ten,[2] and in 1900, it was 20 percent. Today only 1.5 percent of our children die before reaching ten years.
4. Today in Canada and in the United States, both the birth rates and the death rates are essentially the lowest in history. Women are having fewer children and older persons are living longer, so it follows that the percentage of older persons increases. In 1900 twenty percent of the infants could expect to

reach 65 years. The ratio is reversed today: 80 percent of the infants can expect to each 65.

5. In 1900 twenty percent of the U.S. population were immigrants; 20 percent more were children of immigrants. Immigrants were younger persons when they came to U.S. and disproportionately increased the percentage of young persons for that time, and they are now a part of the older population.

6. Women today represent 60 percent of those sixty-five and above. In pioneer days many women literally worked themselves to death with large families, few labor-saving devices in the homes, and poor health services. Many died in childbirth or from complications of childbirth, situations which good health and good medical practices today have virtually eliminated. In United States females began to equal males in total number in the decade of 1940 to 1949. In the 1960-1969 decade the female population sixty-five and above increased 28 percent and the male population 11 percent. This trend continues today. "Women in the sixty-five and older age-group are the fastest-growing segment of the U.S. population. . . . Women are also living much longer than men, a gap in life expectancy which will continue into the next century. The growth in the number of older women is having an enormous impact on society. Yet the needs and achievements of older women have been largely overlooked."[3] In the total U.S. population there are 105 females to 100 males.

At sixty-five there are 140 females to 100 males; at eighty-five and above there are two females for every male.

In their forties males and females in Canada and U.S. are about equal in number. At this point in life the three great killers—diseases of the heart, malignancies, and strokes—move in much more heavily upon males than upon females. These three diseases may affect more females as they increasingly follow the practices of men.

Baby boomers and baby busters
The ten-year period, 1947 to 1956, following World War II is called the "baby boom." Forty-three million children were born in U.S. in those ten years, 20 percent of the population, at a rate of 3.8 children per woman fifteen to forty-four years.[4] This rate has now dropped to 1.9. A rate of 2.1 is required to sustain the population, without immigrants. However, the population in the U.S. continues to grow because the large numbers of "baby boomers" are now having families, albeit, small ones, labeled the "baby busters."

During 1979, there were 1,906,000 deaths in U.S. (8.7 deaths per 1,000 population), the lowest annual death rate ever recorded in this country.

How will the demographic trends affect the church of the future?
1. Church membership will include more and more older persons. The median age (half above and half below) was sixteen years in 1800, 23.4 in 1900, is thirty-one today, and will reach forty in fifty years. In today's congregations statistically one fifth of the members are sixty-five and over. In fifty years this percentage could double unless there is a great increase in the birth rate, which seems unlikely.

2. Young people will be few in numbers. The number of children thirteen

and under in the U.S. has dropped by 7,600,000 since 1970.[5] Many public elementary and secondary schools are closing every year. This has many implications for the future of the church and its educational programs. What can the church do currently to help all age groups deal with this phenomenon and especially help young people not to become disillusioned with the aging process?

3. Ministers will be asked to remain in the active pastorate for longer periods. More women will become leaders and pastors.

4. More and more congregations will be in the hands of women who today represent 60 percent of the sixty-five and above population. Are we now giving women the proper education, the opportunities for experience in church service, and the best chances for the use of their gifts in preparation for greater responsibility? Dr. Robert Bulter, director of the National Institute on Aging, recently noted that "a new kind of older society is evolving and for the main part it is female."[6]

5. The church's future financial resources will be proportionately less than today. Retired persons on the average have only half of their previous income. Also, as the church population becomes increasingly female, it may become financially poorer. Among older persons there are 5.5 times more elderly widows than widowers and poverty is three times more prevalent among older women than older men.[7] Older persons are generally dependent upon fixed incomes and inflation may continue to make such incomes more vulnerable.

6. Usually congregations are "couple"-centered, sometimes forgetting adult singles. The percentage of singles will continue to increase—older widows, husbands and wives who have separated, persons who have never married.

7. Much more time and effort will have to be put forth by the church and the community to understand how older persons react physically and mentally. An Indian proverb says, "I will not criticize my brother until I have walked a mile in his moccasins." Few medical schools give any training in gerontology. However, one medical instructor regularly asks class members to go through a day with plugs in their ears, bandages over their eyes and tape on their fingers to learn something about limitations in hearing, seeing, and feeling and thus be more understanding and sympathetic to those with physical limitations.

NOTES

1. The source of most of these statistics is "Monthly Vital Statistics Report, Provisional Statistics, Annual Summary for the United States, 1979; Births, Deaths, Marriages, Divorces." DHHS Publication No. PHS 81-1120, November 13, 1980.

2. John H. Knowles, MD, "The Struggle to Stay Healthy," *Time*, August 9, 1976.

3. Special Report on Aging: 1979. U.S. Department of Health, Education, and Welfare, NIH Publication No. 79-1907.

4. Matt Clark with Mariana Gasnell, "The Graying of America," *Newsweek*, February 29, 1977.

5. *Ibid.*

6. Tish Sommers and Laurie Shields, *Journal of Home Economics*, Summer 1979, p. 16.

7. *Ibid.*, p. 17.

Appendix 3

This survey form is the work of a Task Force Committee of representatives from each of the operating boards of the Mennonite Church. The form may be used as it is or it may be adapted for special needs of individual Congregations. In many cases personal help will be needed in completing this survey form.

A CONGREGATIONAL SURVEY FORM
(To be completed by persons 65 and over or retirees under 65)

Information given in this survey will be used practically—and in confidence—to help our congregation better respond to your abilities and any needs you may be experiencing. The persons administering this survey will be happy to answer any questions you have as you complete the form.

Your name:_____ Current date:_____

Address: _____ Date of birth:_____
                                                          day   month   year

_____

_____ Telephone:_____

Information about yourself

1. Present residence: retirement facility ____, with family member ____, in own home ____, other (indicate) _____.

2. Single ____, married ____, widowed ____, divorced ____.

3. Employment status: retired ____, semiretired ____, employed full time ____, part time ____.

4. If employed, what is your present job? _____

5. What have been your major life occupations? _____

6. Do you drive a car? yes ____ no ____.

7. Do you own a car? yes ____ no ____. If "no," do you have access to one? yes ____ no ____.

8. Do you have limitations on driving? yes ____ no ____.

9. How many of your children are still living? _____

10. How many children can you phone toll-free or can visit you regularly? ____

11. How many times in the past month have your children visited or phoned you? _____

12. How often are you visited by children living at a distance or by other relatives? _____

13. Can you regularly attend church and other activities? yes ____ no ____. If "no," why not? _____

14. Do you have serious health problems? yes ____ no ____. If "yes," what problems? _____

15. How do you usually spend your time? _____

Information about your gifts and abilities

Would you like to help others part time, voluntarily, or for reasonable pay in some of the following? If yes, check which of the following you would be ready to do (double-check √ √ those services for which you would like payment; identify with an asterisk * those services you are already giving):

16. Homemaker services (go to other person's home)

_____ Cleaning

_____ Cooking

_____ Sewing/mending

_____Other (specify) _____

17. Maintenance and related services

_____ Carpentry

_____ Electrical

_____ Farm labor

_____ General repair work

_____ Heating

_____ Mechanics

_____ Painting

_____ Plumbing

_____Other (specify) _____

18. Personal services

_____ Adoptive grandparents

_____ Baby-sitting

_____ Furnish transportation

_____ Literary sharing (poetry, reading)

_____ Live-in companion

_____Teaching hobbies (specify) _____

19. Professional services

_____ Counseling (specify areas) _____

_____ Financial adviser

_____ Nursing

_____Tutor

_____Other (specify)_____

I would be ready to help (or already am helping) in the mission of our congregation by (√ for willingness; √ √ for services you are already giving):

20. Service to the congregation

_____ Help handicapped, ill, lonely

_____ Keep records

_____ Lead Bible study

_____ Lead worship

_____ Library work

_____ Music (specify)

_____ Prayer ministry

_____ Preaching

_____ Share recollections

_____ Teaching

_____ Visitation

_____ Write letters

_____Other (specify) _____

21. Outreach of the congregation

_____ Bookrack evangelism

_____ Prayer ministry

_____ Prison ministry

_____ Voluntary service (explain kind of service) _____

_____ Other (specify)_____

I would be ready to help (or already am helping) in service to our community by volunteer work in (√ for willingness; √ √ for services you are already giving):

22. Community organizations

_____ Hospital

_____ Library

_____ Meals-on-Wheels

_____ Red Cross

_____ Tutoring

_____ Wheels-to-Meals

_____ Other (specify) _____

23. Individual opportunities

_____ Companion shopper

_____ School aide

_____ Other (specify) _____

Information about your needs

Check each item for which *you feel a need*. Double-check √ √ for a stronger felt need.

24. Financial

_____ Estate planning

_____ Exploration of

     Social Security

_____ Insurance

_____ Investments

_____ Tax information

_____ Other (specify) _____

25. Health

_____ Blood pressure checks

_____ Care of feet

_____ Explanation of medications

_____ Medication

_____ Nursing services at home

____ Personal care (hair, toenails, bathing)

____ Routine blood tests

____ Shots

____Other (specify) _____

26. Legal

____ Legal counsel

____ Protection from fraud

____ Wills

____ Other (specify) _____

27. Nutrition

____ Help shopping

____Meal planning

____ Meal preparation

____ Indicate recent changes in your eating habits: _____

_____

28. Personal

____ Choosing a nursing home

____ Choosing a retirement home

____ Communion at home

____ Decision-making

____ Letter writing

____ Pastoral visits

____ Regular phone calls

____ Spiritual counsel

____ Writing your funeral plans

____ My unmet or partially met needs are: _____

_____

Check each item for which *you feel a need.* Double-check √ √ for a strongly felt need.

29. Seasonal

____ Cleaning house

_____ Home maintenance

_____ Homemaker services

_____ Mowing lawn

_____ Raking leaves

_____ Snow removal

_____ Storm windows

_____ Working garden

_____ Other (specify) _____

30. Transportation

_____ Church

_____ Doctor or dentist

_____ Shopping

_____ To visit out-of-town friend or relative

_____ Other (specify) _____

31 Work

_____ For income

_____ For more planned activity

32. Recreation or pastime

I enjoy _____

I would like to learn to _____

_____

Information to help focus a congregational action plan

33. How could the congregation better help you? _____

34. Are you aware of neighbors or friends of any age who need help? (Tell your interviewers or write their names here) _____

What could you do to help meet their need? _____

How could other church members be of help? _____

35. Would you be interested in informal educational courses or training?_____
In what areas? _____

36. If you had the opportunity, what would you like to do most? Dream a little!

_____

37. How old would you be (*feel*) if you didn't know how old you are? _____

38. What are your concerns for your future? Fears?   _____

39. What other suggestions do you have to help your congregation to be aware of aging persons' opportunities and needs? _____

_____

40. What are your feelings about completing this survey form? _____

_____

Appendix 4

Ardean Goertzen worked with the author for seven months in 1975. He personally visited fifty congregations in Northern Indiana. This glossary was developed to cover discussions with church leaders in the congregations visited.

SERVICES WITH OLDER PERSONS: A GLOSSARY

1. ADVOCACY—Generally, this whole area implies some kind of structure that mediates between needs and resources.

    a. *Assisting persons* in securing health, food, and other services they are entitled to. This could be handled by a committee that keeps elderly persons informed of rights and privileges, helps in acquiring food stamps and other such resources that might be rightfully theirs.

    b. *Monitoring of programs* in the church and community involves the whole area of working at watching, observing, and checking on the needs of the elderly and on the quality and fidelity of the programs that do exist. Any structure that keeps tabs on resources and needs and actively mediates between the two would be a monitoring program.

    c. *Communication services* to government at the local, state, and federal level to speak out on behalf of the elderly is a way of voicing the concerns of the elderly regarding legislation to appropriate resources on their behalf.

    d. *Project FIND* (Friendless, Isolated, Needy, and Disabled) is a federal advocacy program sponsored by the National Council on Aging under the Office of Economic Opportunity. Its goal is to locate elderly poor who are what the word "FIND" implies, to identify their individual needs and problems, and to determine their skills and resources; it then refers such individuals to the appropriate agency or agencies to help meet their particular needs.

2. COMMUNICATION SERVICES—Information is disseminated by various agencies and media concerning programs, services, and goods of special interest to the elderly. This might be through church bulletins, church newsletters, or a directory of skills and resources of those in the congregation. For example, the bulletin or newsletter would carry information on a new program such as Supplemental Security Income bill passed by Congress and information on how and where such aid could be applied for, by whom, and what qualifications might be needed to be eligible.

3. CONGREGATIONAL AND PASTORAL MINISTRY—

    a. *Pastoral care* by home visitation of elderly is an important area and one that should be systematically worked at. A pastor may find it difficult or impossible to make the rounds, so someone should be trained to give such care if possible.

    b. *Worship and religious publications* could be geared to the elderly on occasion. Many feel sermons are directed too much at youth or the family. Articles in publications are often biased the same way.

c. *Work with the bereaved and dying.* This is a familiar area for pastors, but there are always ways to work at being more fully present and sensitive to those who need to do grief work because of loss in whatever way or form.

d. *Large-print books,* Bibles, devotional materials, and hymnals are excellent aids for those with impaired vision. Bibles such as the Good News and KJV are in large print. Also, the *Upper Room* is now available in large print and should be made available in churches for purchase at cost or discount to the elderly.

e. *Inventory center of skills and resources.* This is a simple research instrument that can be used to research the available skills and resources of members, including the elderly. After the facts have been gathered, they can be published in a directory. Thus, if a person needed to have help with fixing an appliance, for example, he could consult the directory for information on who might be of help to him. Need is linked with skilled resources to the benefit of both.

f. *Planned housing by efficiency apartments.* This refers to the church taking responsibility to provide efficiency apartments (remodeled from larger houses to fit the needs of those elderly who might live in them more economically as a group). The goal is to provide a financial break, as well as allow for more intimate living, companionship, pooling of interests and resources, while still allowing for a degree of independence.

g. *Elderly with the time and skill* can help the pastor with writing, research, filing, visitation, teaching, church records, mimeographing, make and receive phone calls, address envelopes, and such projects. Many have time and skill to give. By taking inventory of these, much of the administrative busywork of running a church could be creatively handled by the elderly to the mutual benefit of both.

4. COOPERATIVE PURCHASING—Group buying plans with wholesale merchants is one way to give financial breaks to the elderly on fixed incomes. The church has space and facilities that could accommodate a food co-op where food could be brought, divided into purchase request lots, and picked up. Labor required for purchasing and sorting could be on a volunteer basis.

5. COUNSELING—

a. *Pastoral counseling* is just beginning to take into consideration the overall concerns of the aged and those of middle age who need help in thinking ahead to retirement. Vocational (full- or part-time jobs) and referral counseling knowledge should be current and available in this area. Older persons with skills could be trained to help counsel others. Remarriage of middle-aged and older persons should be an important area of focus.

b. *Training and functioning of volunteer congregational counselors.* Many laymen, including the elderly, could help with counseling in many areas, if they were given some encouragement and supervision. Some might be professionals (lawyers, e.g.) whose expertise could be used to counsel others along legal lines. Some may have listening skills and an attempt could be made to use these as broadly as possible.

c. *Counseling services* for legal and financial matters, filling out forms such as Social Security supplemental income, and the like need attention. Technical jargon and red tape keep many elderly from their rightful benefits. Being sensitive to need in this area and having facts on hand could help many toward securing benefits. Pastors or those trained to give advice in special areas including financial planning, transportation, and housing could be helpful.

6. EDUCATION—

a. *Adult education.* Churches have facilities (space and equipment) that could be used as centers to provide programmed learning along vocational lines, as well as offerings in communication skills, hobbies, and courses on the Bible and other areas of interest. Teachers and teacher aides can be used in the program, and resources of the local schools should not be overlooked. Vocation and general interest courses should be available to the elderly in local high schools, and churches might take a role in facilitating this so that it becomes a reality.

b. *Library clubs.* Aides are needed to help in libraries, including the church library, to file, catalog, stack books, and do a host of needed things.

c. *Study clubs.* Book discussion and study based on topics of current interest and need are excellent educational opportunities. Leadership is important in this area. Pastors should be informed about what is going on and what possibilities might be offered.

d. *Development of curriculum materials* for older persons. Such curriculum material would take into account the psychological, sociological, biological, and economical, aspects of aging and ways to cope with the intensified needs that come with old age.

e. *The resources and skills of the elderly themselves* are too often overlooked. Their accumulated skills and experience could be creatively used on a consultation basis in courses at anywhere from the grade school to the college level. Many could make good apprentice supervisors. For example, at a church college retired persons with creative cooking skills and interests help teach in the home economics department on a consultative basis.

7. EMPLOYMENT—

a. *An employment agency* could be a possibility in any church to help elderly find work along lines of their interests. It would assist in information gathering and referral plus helping the person apply and get adjusted to a new job or second vocation.

b. *Employment in voluntary agencies.* Many agencies, such as the Retired Senior Volunteer Program (RSVP), hospitals, home services, and schools need volunteer help. Bookrack evangelism is an example of one area where volunteer help can further the church's work and challenge the creativity of those persons involved.

c. *Green Thumb/Green Light.* Sponsored by the National Farmers Union under a grant from the U.S. Department of Labor, these programs provide limited employment to low-income elderly, aged 55 or older, in rural areas. In Green Thumb, retired men are employed three days a week to beautify public areas. Green Light women employees serve as aides in community services through special outreach projects, and help to make these services available to the handicapped, sick, and elderly shut-ins.

d. *Score, Vista, Peace Corps,* teacher corps, census takers, and weather observers are all examples of government-sponsored job programs in which the elderly can serve with pay. Under the denominational mission boards there are programs such as Voluntary Service and relief work. Also, there are job areas in the Veterans' Administration which need volunteers to work in hospitals around the nation in areas such as writing, doing errands, reading, feeding patients, and recreational activities, mostly for the elderly retired.

8. EXTENDED CARE FACILITIES—

a. *Nursing homes.* There are many ways and levels at which churches might be involved. These might include programs of spiritual nurture, regular visitation, help with various therapies like arts and crafts or helping to start some if such programs are not available. Those members of the church who are living in nursing homes should be given special consideration and care.

b. *Hospital extended care units.* These provide nursing care of a more intensive nature than nursing homes for the aged, but not as intensive as the hospital itself. Usually, the extended care unit is part of the hospital and provides a place for those whose convalescence takes longer and those who need special supervision and therapy (such as physical therapy) which the hospital offers.

9. HEALTH—

a. *Health education.* Instructions in this area could meet needs in various areas including nutrition ("You Are What You Eat"), menu planning, shopping tips, and sound meal preparation. Physiological and emotional aspects of health, exercising properly, could also be taught and emphasized. Regular physical exams for all could be stressed, as well as education to expose health fakes and frauds, swindlers, quacks, and fraudulent advertising which plays on fears especially relating to the elderly. The educational program could also deal with matters of public policy relating to health, health legislation, and current events in the health field.

b. *Health screening.* This could be done by a team consisting of a physician in charge, a public health nurse, social worker, and family health worker. Evaluation and review of medical histories would group persons into areas of related need so they could more adequately help each other and be helped by the resources of the community at large.

c. *Home health service and delivery.* While the functions of homemakers have usually been oriented to care of the household (dusting, washing, cleaning, etc.), and while those of home health aides have been oriented to care of the patient (helping with physical therapy or administration of medicine), many of their tasks overlap. Workers trained to perform these jobs can give a variety of services and make possible flexibility in individual treatment plans. They can also help maximize the use of all community resources. Care administered at home is almost always cheaper than in an institutional bed.

d. *Medical and dental service* information and availability of these at the convenience of the elderly. Information on medical and dental services, health clinics, services offered by hospitals, and the like, is available to persons through pamphlets and other literature. Transportation can be provided for those who cannot otherwise make it to such places of service.

10. HOMEMAKER SERVICES—Services to shut-ins can help older persons maintain independence at home by offering services such as hot meals, repairs, light laundry, and cleaning. Aides could help care workers and county nurses and could volunteer through such programs as RSVP, SCORE, VS, and Peace Corps. Such services would contribute to the health and functioning of the person and prevent costly admissions and re-admissions to institutions. It would make possible earlier discharges from hospitals and nursing homes, thus saving vast amounts of money for all.

11. HOUSING—

a. *Retirement hotels.* These accommodations allow for near-complete independence because of services provided. These include room service, RN service, transportation, laundry service, and so on in a hotel-like atmosphere with a one- or two-bedroom apartment provision.

b. *Retirement village.* Such villages offer independent apartment rental with recreational and health facilities, arts and crafts center, nursing and special room service when needed.

c. *Midtown manors.* These provide low-cost apartment rental with apartments located close together to provide for mutual aid and convenience. Most are government subsidized.

d. *Government subsidized housing apartment complexes.* These are available to the elderly for as little as one fourth of their annual income. The church might see what it could do to encourage use of such low-rent housing.

12. INTERGENERATIONAL RELATIONS—

a. *Foster Grandparent Program.* The Administration on Aging funds and administrates this program under which low-income persons, aged 60 or over, are employed to give love and attention to institutionalized and other needy children. The Foster Grandparents work an average of 20 hours per week and are paid at least the federal minimum wage. They also receive payment during orientation and in-service training and a transportation allowance. They are provided with uniforms and a daily meal.

b. *Foster Teen Program.* Teenagers in this program could be encouraged to adopt a grandparent (in case they did not have one to relate to) who is shut in at home or in a nursing home. Teens would keep up correspondence, visit regularly, and provide wheelchair rides, excursions in the summer, and so forth.

c. *Intergenerational educational experiences* are available in Sunday school situations in which such interaction and needs as exist within the group would be worked at. Topics could focus on family life, conflict resolution, and related Bible studies. High schoolers might do oral history projects by interviewing the elderly of the community on cassette, thereby building up an oral history on the local community. Pioneering models of education in the church such as this and others should be encouraged.

d. *A youth-sponsored senior citizen banquet* could help bridge gaps where they exist. Youth would honor senior citizens by serving them at the banquet and giving them a place in the planning and production of the program, which would itself focus on the achievements and experiences of the elderly.

13. INCOME MAINTENANCE—Many elderly need special financial assistance either on a regular or emergency basis through deacons or emergency funds. Many elderly have only their Social Security and this itself is hardly enough to subsist on, to say nothing of various emergencies caused by poor health and the like.

14. LEGAL—

a. *Legal counseling* given by employed or volunteer attorneys who could assist with filling out of legal forms and reading and interpreting of legal documents. The poor elderly are especially in need of this, since they often do not have the financial means to pay attorney fees and often also are unable to read and interpret important legal documents pertaining to their welfare in such areas as selling a house, purchasing and renting a new facility and land, leases, contracts of all kinds, insurance, financial plans, Social Security, SSI, and the like. Legal checkups should be encouraged by someone appointed for just such a service to make sure it gets done.

b. *Counseling on tax forms.* Many elderly are given special exemptions and should know about them. Consideration should also be given to proper filling out of income, estate, and gift-income forms.

c. *Making out wills and trusts* to church and conference institutions is one phase of responsibility in adult stewardship that should be encouraged in some structured fashion. This could be handled by an informed pastor or lawyer and should be part of good stewardship emphasis and practice.

d. *Legal aid* is a way of making special funds available to the elderly poor who may need legal counsel but would have to pay for it, and otherwise could not afford it.

e. *Guardianship and conservatorship* programs are legal programmed ways of handling and administrating the estate of someone under age or otherwise incompetent.

15. NUTRITIONAL—

a. *Nutritional counseling and education.* A program to encourage proper eating (and dieting) and education concerning nutritional needs and how to meet them. Health depends on the right intake of calories, carbohydrates, proteins, minerals, and vitamins. How best to select food and prepare it, and how to meet basic needs could be emphasized.

b. *Food buying guide service.* Food guides such as those published by Action for Independent Maturity (AIM) contain valuable tips on buying and preparing food to save money and eat nutritionally. These could be made available in churches along with other literature.

c. *Meals on Wheels.* A program providing hot meals to older shut-ins who can no longer cook for themselves. The program may be federally funded through the AOA or by local funds. It is administered by churches and nursing homes, schools, or wherever facilities for preparation and processing are adequate to meet health and other standards. Meals are then taken to homes by volunteers, thus providing daily contact with the person as well. The program helps the elderly to maintain independence longer.

d. *Wheels to Meals.* A program providing transportation for those needing it and hot meals at a central location (church, school, senior center). In some of the programs, the elderly take pride in participating in the preparation and serving of the meal. The program provides not only food, but also socialization around meals and programs of a group nature. This program provides, in most cases, for at least 3-4 nutritional meals per week for those who sometimes do not care to cook at home because they simply do not enjoy eating alone.

16. REFERRAL—This refers primarily to a clearinghouse function to help older persons find needed services not provided by the church. Referrals may be made in many areas depending on the nature of the problem or need. Referrals to mental health institutions, county welfare, and Alcoholics Anonymous are examples of pre-counseling which help people get quality professional help for their particular needs. Referrals may also, of course, be made to members on the basis of outstanding resources of people within the congregation itself.

17. REHABILITATION-RETRAINING—

a. *Vocational training workshops.* With current mobility and job fluctuation, this program would use experts in various specialized fields to train persons for new jobs in areas of need and interest. Many elderly want to learn skills (carpentry, glass cutting, ceramics, etc.) to provide supplemental income to their budgets. This program would add a dimension of meaning in work and dignity to their lives.

b. *Senior day care centers.* These centers provide a meeting place with tools and resources where people can be involved in creative ways to retrain themselves or just to learn a new hobby and fellowship with others. Many centers may provide a variety of services and material resources and machines for wood and steel lathe work, carving, looms, spinning, needlecrafts, etc.

     c. *County courthouse ministry.* Pioneering work needs to be done in this area. The possibilities for a supportive and enabling ministry to all those who come here for help, as well as those who work at giving that help, is a possibility and needs to be explored—including a ministry at the county jail.

18. PRE-RETIREMENT TRAINING—This area could cover such items as classes or workshops (even retreats) geared to younger and middle-aged adults to help them plan realistically for retirement. Emphasis here is on learning to plan ahead for financial security in some form, use of leisure-time activities, meaningful second vocations if necessary, service for the church and community, travel, and continued education. Good retirement training is never limited to financial security, and the sooner planning begins, the better!

19. SELF-DEVELOPMENT/SELF-EMPOWERMENT—Programs designed to make the elderly self-sufficient so that they might represent themselves and the interests of other elderly to various kinds of officials and power groups through provision of space, funds, equipment, and one's expertise is important here. Being able to speak up and organize one's interests and those of others with similar interests around causes is significant for our day of power politics. Being able to represent one's interests at the local, state, or federal level is much needed, and especially among the elderly. This would help those causes unique to the needs and interests of older persons.

20. TELEPHONE REASSURANCE—

     a. *First,* a committee could be responsible for calling the elderly shut-ins on a special line or phone which would also be used by the elderly to call for help. This would imply personnel staff to take such calls and train others to do calling from the center provided for such a purpose. Often older persons have no one to check on them or just to keep in touch, thus raising the threat of being left helpless in case of an accident of whatever type. For example, in case of a stroke that might leave the person helpless, a non-answering of a phone call would indicate trouble and the problem would be checked immediately.

     b. *Volunteers* could also call from their home to the home of an elderly person who needs reassuring and checking on, or just to have a brief visit to cheer the day. The parties involved in each case would call at an agreed-upon time to reassure each other each day. This program is not only reassuring for those called, but to the caller and family of the one receiving reassurance as well. This program has already helped prevent many tragedies and deaths each year.

21. TRANSPORTATION—

a. *Transportation* arranged for elderly who cannot drive to come to worship services. This can usually be handled by a special committee that organizes transportation for those who cannot drive, for whatever reason, and those who can offer such a service.

b. *Transportation* can likewise be arranged for elderly people to help them get around in general for shopping, paying bills, getting to the doctor, drugstore, dentist, etc. Here a phone number or need list would be made out and people with time and transport available would volunteer to drive older persons around as needed.

c. *FISH.* FISH is an ecumenical lay ministry movement with no national structure. Chapters are being organized in many communities to work toward filling needs as they arise and exist within the community. FISH is providing a diversity of services such as meals on wheels, emergency baby-sitting, companionship to elderly, battered children's centers, clothing closets, crises intervention, disaster relief, transportation, errands, family adoption, and a host of other services.

22. VISITING-COMPANIONSHIP—

a. *Adoption of older person* by family to visit regularly. Many elderly have no family and this is one way the church could work at being the extended family. Members can then assume the same kind of care for the elderly person as they would toward one of their own family members.

b. *Youth groups could share* in a variety of ways with the elderly who are shut-ins and living in homes for the aged. Various ways of socializing around games and food are also good things to try and do. Where possible, physical recreation can also be enjoyed together. Youth can share from their contemporary "world" and experiences in programmed ways through slides, skits, as well as individually.

c. *Newsletter to "forgotten" persons.* Volunteers in this case would write to people who may receive no mail—not even advertisements. Everyone needs to be remembered and to receive something in the mail that says, "I care about you." Getting people to commit themselves to write a letter or more per week is one way of structuring this to insure that it will get done.

d. *Live-in companion.* One widow or widower can move in with another to help meet each other's companionship needs as well as share in meeting costs of housing, utilities, food, and other items.

23. WIDOWED PERSONS—Plan programs uniquely geared to the needs of widows, widowers, and the handicapped. For example, a group of widows or widowers might be organized for mutual support and for dialoguing on subjects such as remarriage or the problems of living alone after the loss of a spouse.

Selected Bibliography

BOOKS

Barks, Herbert B. *Prime Time: Moving into Middle Age with Style,* Nashville: Thomas Nelson, 1978.

Bischof, Ledford J. *Adult Psychology,* New York: Harper and Row, 1969.

Bradford, Leland B., and Bradford, Martha I., *Retirement: Coping with Emotional Upheavels.* Chicago: Nelson-Hall, 1979.

Butler, Robert, and Lewis, Myrna. *Aging and Mental Health,* St. Louis: C. V. Mosby Co., 1972.

Clinebell, Howard J. *Growth Counseling for Mid-Year Couples.* Philadelphia: Fortress Press, 1977.

Clingan, Donald F. *Aging Persons in the Community of Faith.* St. Louis: Christian Board of Education, 1975.

Comfort, Alex. *A Good Age.* New York: Crown, 1976.

Cook, Thomas C., and Thorsen, James. *Spiritual Well-Being of the Elderly.* Springfield, Ill.: Charles C. Thomas, 1980.

Cousins, Norman. *Anatomy of an Illness as Perceived by a Patient.* New York: W. W. Norton, 1979.

Curtin, Sharon R. *Nobody Ever Died of Old Age: In Praise of Old People,* Boston: Atlantic Monthly Press Book, Little, Brown and Co., 1972.

Deeken, Alfons. *Growing Old and How to Cope with It.* New York: Paulist Press, 1972.

Downs, Hugh. *Thirty Dirty Lies About Old.* Niles, Ill.: Argus Communications, 1979.

Fischer, David Hackett. *Growing Old in America.* New York: Oxford University Press, 1977.

Fish, Harriet A. *Activities Program for Senior Citizens.* West Nyack, N.Y.: Parker Publishing Co., 1971.

Gourlay, Jack. *Life After 65.* New York: Associated Press, 1974.

Hamilton, William B., and Reid, Helen F. *A Hospice Handbook.* Grand Rapids: Eerdmans, 1980.

Howe, Reuel L. *How to Stay Younger—While Growing Older.* Waco, Texas: Word Books, 1974.

Hunter, Woodrow H. *Preparation for Retirement.* Ann Arbor: University of Michigan Press, 1976.

_____. *Retirement Education Leader's Manual.* Ann Arbor: University of Michigan Press, 1980.

Kubler-Ross, Elizabeth, *On Death and Dying.* New York: Macmillan, 1972.

Le Fevre, Carol, and Le Fevre, Perry. *Aging and the Human Spirit: A Reader in Religion and Gerontology.* Chicago: Exploration Press, 1981.

Lehman, Harold D. *In Praise of Leisure.* Scottdale, Pa.: Herald Press, 1974.

Moberg, David O. *Spiritual Well-Being.* Washington, D.C.: University Press of America, 1979.

Neufeldt, A. H. *Commission on Aging: A Survey.* Saskatchewan, Canada: Mennonite Central Committee, 1974.

Rogers, Dorothy. *The Adult Years.* Englewood Cliffs, N.J.: Prentice Hall, 1979.

Schmitt, Abraham. *Dialogue with Death.* Waco, Texas: Word Books, 1976.

Shedd, Charles W. *Then God Created Grandparents and It Was Very Good.* Garden City, N.Y.: Doubleday, 1978.

Start, Clarissa. *On Becoming a Widow.* St. Louis: Concordia, 1973.

Stoddard, Sandol. *The Hospice Movement—A Better Way of Caring for the Dying.* Briarcliff Manor, N.Y.: Stein and Day Publishers, 1978.

Tilberg, Cedric W. *The Fullness of Life.* New York: Lutheran Church in America, 1980.

Tournier, Paul. *Learn to Grow Old.* New York: Harper and Row, 1971.

Woodruff, Diana S. and Birren, James E. *Aging: Scientific Perspectives and Social Issues.* New York: D. Van Nostrand, 1975.

Yoder, Jonathan G. *Healing: Prayer or Pills?* Scottdale, Pa.: Herald Press, 1975.

Ziegler, Jesse H., editor. *Theological Education.* Special Issue, Winter 1980, sponsored by National Interfaith Coalition on Aging, P.O. Box 130, Vandalia, Ohio, 1980.

MAGAZINES AND OTHER MATERIALS

Aging. U.S. Department of Health, Education, and Welfare, Social and Rehabilitation Service—Administration on Aging; U.S. Printing Office, Public Documents, Washington, D.C.

Canadian Institute of Religion and Gerontology (newsletter). 296 Lawrence Avenue East, Toronto, Ontario M4N 1T7.

Modern Maturity. American Association of Retired Persons, P.O. Box 729, Long Beach, California 90801.

NRTA Journal. National Retired Teachers Association, 701 N. Montgomery St., Ojai, California 93023.

Perspective on Aging. National Council on the Aging, Inc., 1828 L Street N.W. Washington DC 20036.

Retirement Guides. American Association of Retired Persons, 215 Long Beach Blvd., Long Beach, CA 90801.

The Gerontologist. Gerontological Society, 1 Dupont Circle, Washington, DC 20036.

50 Plus. 99 Garden Street, Marion, Ohio 43302.

Two good Canadian sources for materials on aging are:
Office on Aging, Homes for the Aged Branch
Ministry of Community and Social Services
Hepburn Block, Parliament Buildings
Toronto 182, Ontario

New Horizons, National Office*
Department of National Health and Welfare
General Purpose Building
Tunneys Pasture
Ottawa, Ontario K1A 1B3

FILM CATALOGS ON AGING

Films on Aging
    Administration on Aging and HEW
    Superintendent of Documents
    U.S. Gov. Printing Office
    Washington, D.C. 20402

About aging: A Catalogue of Films
    Ethel Percy Andrus Gerontology Center
    University of Southern California
    Los Angeles, Calif.

Most province, state, university, and city libraries have films on aging which
    can be rented. The Mennonite Board of Congregational Ministries, Box
    1245, Elkhart, IN 46515, has a number of films on aging which can be
    rented at a reasonable fee.

---

*Each province of Canada has a regional New Horizons office.

The Author

Tilman R. Smith has served as director of studies and programs for the aging for the Mennonite Church at Mennonite Board of Missions, Elkhart, Indiana, during the past decade.

Church activities on the local, conference, and national levels have been given top priority in Smith's life. He served his local congregation for more than twenty years as Sunday school superintendent and almost as long as director of church music. He was appointed by Illinois Mennonite Conference as its representative to the Mennonite Board of Education, Mennonite Mutual Aid, as chairman of the first Mennonite Disaster Service Committee, and as member of the committee which purchased the site for Camp Menno Haven. He served the Mennonite Church for twelve years as a trustee of Schowalter Foundation, Inc., Newton, Kansas.

Tilman Smith was professor of education at Goshen College, 1969-71; director of an institutional self-study at Eastern Mennonite College, 1968-69; president of Hesston College, 1959-68; vice-president of Ulrich Manufacturing Co., Roanoke, Illinois, 1947-49; and first a teacher and later an administrator in the Illinois public schools, 1928-47, 1949-59.

In his role as denominational gerontologist, Smith has served as a resource person for many lectures, consultations, and workshops, and has engaged in extensive research and writing. He is the author of *Boards: Purposes, Organization, Procedures* (Herald Press, 1978). His articles have appeared in *Mennonite Weekly Review, Gospel Herald, Forum, Sharing, Festival Quarterly,* and other publications.

Tilman and Louella (Schertz) Smith are members of Goshen College Mennonite Church, Goshen, Indiana, and parents of five grown children: Carolyn, Marian, John, Eleanor, and Stanley.

In 1965 Bethany College, Lindsborg, Kansas, conferred an honorary degree, Doctor of Humane Letters (LHD) upon Tilman Smith, the first non-Lutheran to be so honored. The citation read in part: "You have given outstanding leadership to higher education, you have joined others in supporting ecumenicity in the churchly activities of higher education, you have been spokesman and leader of the faith of your fathers, the Old Mennonites."